Software Architecture of Online Shopping Systems

-- Structure-Behavior Coalescence Method for Model Singularity --

William S. Chao

Structure-Behavior Coalescence

Software Architecture = Software Structure + Software Behavior

CONTENTS

PREFACE

A software system is complex that it comprises multiple views such as strategy/version n, strategy/version n+1, concept, analysis, design, implementation, structure, behavior and input/output data views. Accordingly, a software system is defined as a set of interacting components forming an integrated whole of that system's multiple views.

Since structure and behavior views are the two most prominent ones among multiple views, integrating the structure and behavior views is a method for integrating multiple views of a software system. In other words, structure-behavior coalescence (SBC) is a single model (model singularity) approach which results in the integration of multiple views. Therefore, it is concluded that the SBC architecture is so proper to model the multiple views of a software system.

In this book, we use the SBC architecture description language (SBC-ADL) to describe and represent the software architecture of the online shopping system. An architecture description language is a special kind of system model used in defining the architecture of a system. SBC-ADL uses six fundamental diagrams to formally grasp the essence of a system and its details at the same time. These diagrams are: a) architecture hierarchy diagram, b) framework diagram, c) component operation diagram, d) component connection diagram, e) structure-behavior coalescence diagram and f) interaction flow diagram.

Software architecture is on the rise. By this book's introduction and elaboration of the software architecture of the online shopping system, all readers may understand clearly how the SBC-ADL helps architects effectively perform architecting, in order to productively construct the fruitful software architecture.

ABOUT THE AUTHOR

Dr. William S. Chao is the CEO & founder of SBC Architecture International®. SBC (Structure-Behavior Coalescence) architecture is a systems architecture which demands the integration of systems structure and systems behavior of a system. SBC architecture applies to hardware architecture, software architecture, enterprise architecture, knowledge architecture and thinking architecture. The core theme of SBC architecture is: Architecture = Structure + Behavior.

William S. Chao received his bachelor degree (1976) in telecommunication engineering and master degree (1981) in information engineering, both from the National Chiao-Tung University, Taiwan. From 1976 till 1983, he worked as an engineer at Chung-Hwa Telecommunication Company, Taiwan.

William S. Chao received his master degree (1985) in information science and Ph.D. degree (1988) in information science, both from the University of Alabama at Birmingham, USA. From 1988 till 1991, he worked as a computer scientist at GE Research and Development Center, Schenectady, New York, USA.

Dr. William S. Chao has been teaching at National Sun Yat-Sen University, Taiwan since 1992 and now serves as the president of Association of Enterprise Architects, Taiwan Chapter. His research covers: systems architecture, hardware architecture, software architecture, enterprise architecture, knowledge architecture and thinking architecture.

PART I: BASIC CONCEPTS

Chapter 1: Introduction to Online Shopping Systems

The online shopping system is a highly distributed world wide web-based system that provides services for purchasing items such as books or clothes. In the online shopping system, customers can request to order one or more items from the supplier. The customer provides personal details, such as address and credit card information. This information is stored in a customer account. If the credit card is valid, then a delivery order is created and sent to the supplier. The supplier checks the available inventory, confirms the order, and enters a planned shipping date. When the order is shipped, the customer is notified and the customer's credit card account is charged.

Behaviors of the online shopping system consist of: a) *Browse_Catalog* behavior, b) *Make_Order_Request* behavior, c) *Process_Delivery_Order* behavior, d) *Confirm_Shipment_and_Bill_Customer* behavior and e) *View_Order* behavior.

1-1 Behavior of Browse_Catalog

The online shopping system allows a customer to browse the catalog and make a selection from the catalog.

In the behavior of *Browse_Catalog*, a customer shall use the *Customer_UI* component to view various catalog from a given supplier's catalog and selects items from the catalog.

1-2 Behavior of Make_Order_Request

The online shopping system allows a customer to enter an order request to purchase catalog items. The customer's credit card is checked for validity and sufficient credit to pay for the requested catalog items.

In the behavior of *Make_Order_Request*, the system shall use the *Customer_UI* component to accept an order request from the customer and display the order information to the customer.

1-3 Behavior of Process_Delivery_Order

The online shopping system allows a supplier to request a delivery order, determines that the inventory is available to fulfill the order, and displays the order.

In the behavior of *Process_Delivery_Order*, a supplier shall use the *Supplier_UI* component to view the delivery order and make the appropriate inventory reservation.

1-4 Behavior of Confirm_Shipment_and_Bill_Customer

The online shopping system allows the supplier to prepare the shipment manually and confirms that the order is ready for shipment. When the order is shipped, the customer is notified and the customer's credit card account is charged.

In the behavior of *Confirm_Shipment_and_Bill_Customer*, a supplier shall use the *Supplier_UI* component to initiate the shipping and billing affairs.

1-5 Behavior of View_Order

The online shopping system allows the customer to view the details of the delivery order.

In the behavior of *View_Order*, a customer shall use the *Customer_UI* component to view the order information.

Chapter 2: Introduction to Software Architecture

A software system comprises multiple views such as strategy/version n, strategy/version n+1, concept, analysis, design, implementation, structure, behavior and input/output data views. A systems model is required to describe and represent all these multiple views.

The systems model describes and represents the system multiple views possibly using two different approaches. The first one is the non-architectural approach and the second one is the architectural approach. The non-architectural approach respectively picks a model for each view. The architectural approach, instead of picking many heterogeneous and separated models, will use only one single multiple views coalescence (MVC) model.

In general, MVC architecture is synonymous with the software architecture. Since structure and behavior views are the two most prominent ones among multiple views, integrating the structure and behavior views becomes a superb approach for integrating multiple views of a system. In other words, structure-behavior coalescence (SBC) leads to the coalescence of multiple views. Therefore, we conclude that SBC architecture is also synonymous with the software architecture.

2-1 Multiple Views of a Software System

In general, a software system is extremely complex that it consists of several evolution&motivation views such as strategy/version n and strategy/version n+1 views; it also consists of various multi-level (hierarchical) views such as concept, analysis, design and implementation views; it also consists of many systemic views such as structure, behavior and input/output data views [Kend10, Pres09, Somm06].

Figure 2-1 shows that in a software system all these strategy/version n, strategy/version n+1, concept, analysis, design, implementation, structure, behavior and input/output data views represent the multiple views of a software system.

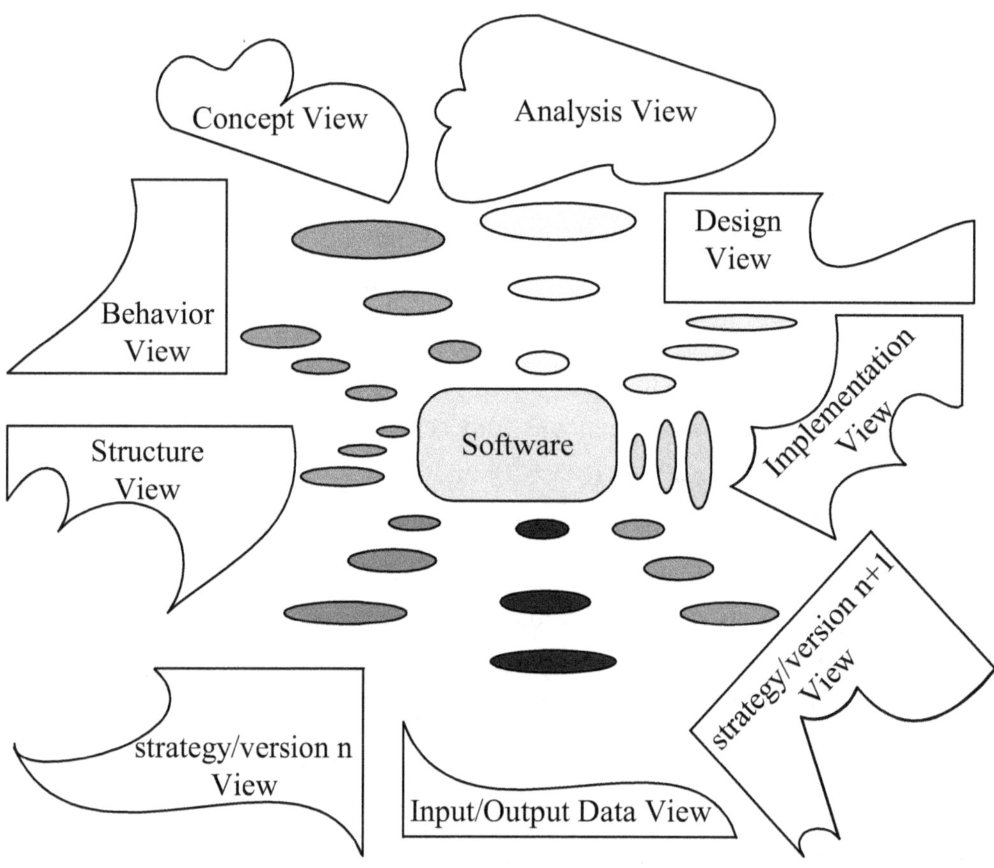

Figure 2-1. Multiple Views of a Software System

Among the above multiple views, the structure and behavior views are perceived as the two prominent ones. The structure view focuses on the software structure which is described by components and their composition while the behavior view concentrates on the software behavior which involves interactions (or handshakes) among the external environment's actors and components. Strategy/version n, strategy/version n+1, concept, analysis, design, implementation and input/output data views are considered to be other views as shown in Figure 2-2.

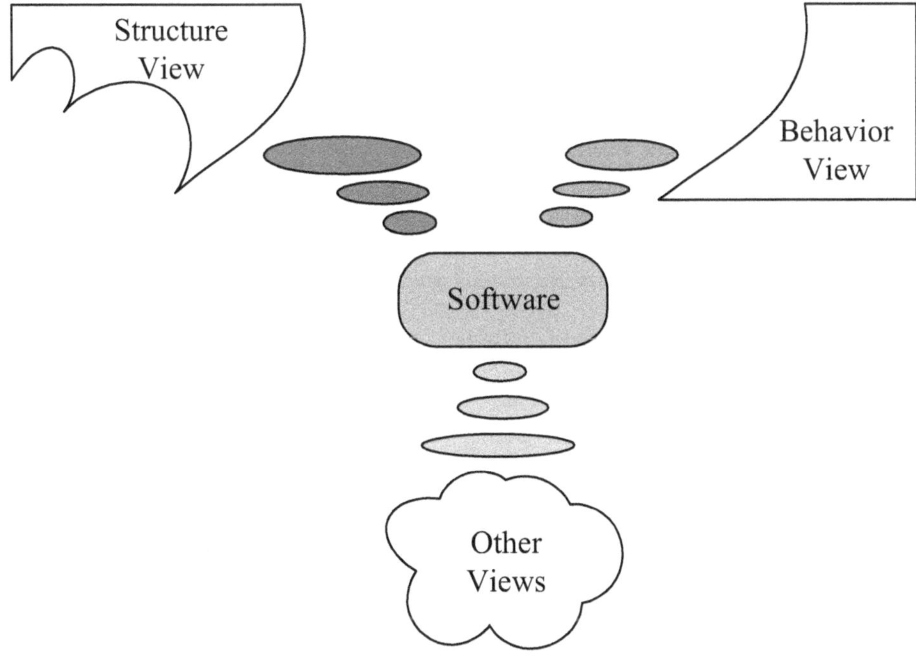

Figure 2-2. Structure, Behavior and Other Views

Accordingly, a software system is defined in Figure 2-3 as an integrated whole of that software system's multiple views, i.e., structure, behavior and other views, embodied in its assembled components, their interactions (or handshakes) with each other and the environment. Components are sometimes named as non-aggregated systems, parts, entities, objects and building blocks [Chao14a, Chao14b, Chao14c, Chec99].

A software system, hopefully is an integrated whole of that software system's multiple views, i.e., structure, behavior, and other views, embodied in its assembled components, their interrelationships with each other and the environment.

Figure 2-3. Definition of a Software System

Since multiple views are embodied in a software system's assembled components which belong to the software structure, they shall not exist alone. Multiple views must be loaded on the software structure just like a cargo is loaded on a ship as shown in Figure 2-4. There will be no multiple views if there is no software structure. Stand-alone multiple views are not meaningful.

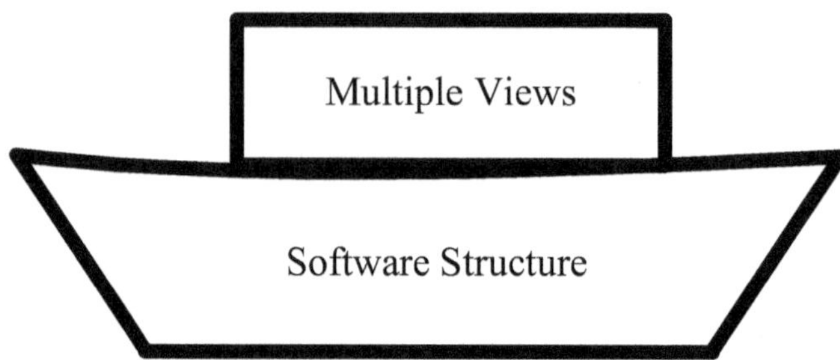

Figure 2-4. Multiple Views Must be Loaded on the Software Structure

2-2 Non-Architectural Approach versus Architectural Approach

A software system is exceptionally complex that it includes multiple views such as strategy/version n, strategy/version n+1, concept, analysis, design, implementation, structure, behavior and input/output data views.

The software systems model describes and represents the system multiple views possibly using two different approaches. The first one is the non-architectural approach and the second one is the architectural approach.

The non-architectural approach, also known as the model multiplicity approach [Dori95, Dori02, Dori16], respectively picks a model for each view as shown in Figure 2-5, the strategy/version n view has the strategy/version n model, the strategy/version n+1 view has the strategy/version n+1 model, the concept view has the concept model, the analysis view has the analysis model, the design view has the design model, the implementation view has the implementation model, the structure view has the structure model, the behavior view has the behavior model, and the input/output data view has the input/output data model. These multiple models are separated, always inconsistent with each other, and then become the primary cause of model multiplicity problems [Dori95, Dori02, Dori16, Pele02, Sode03].

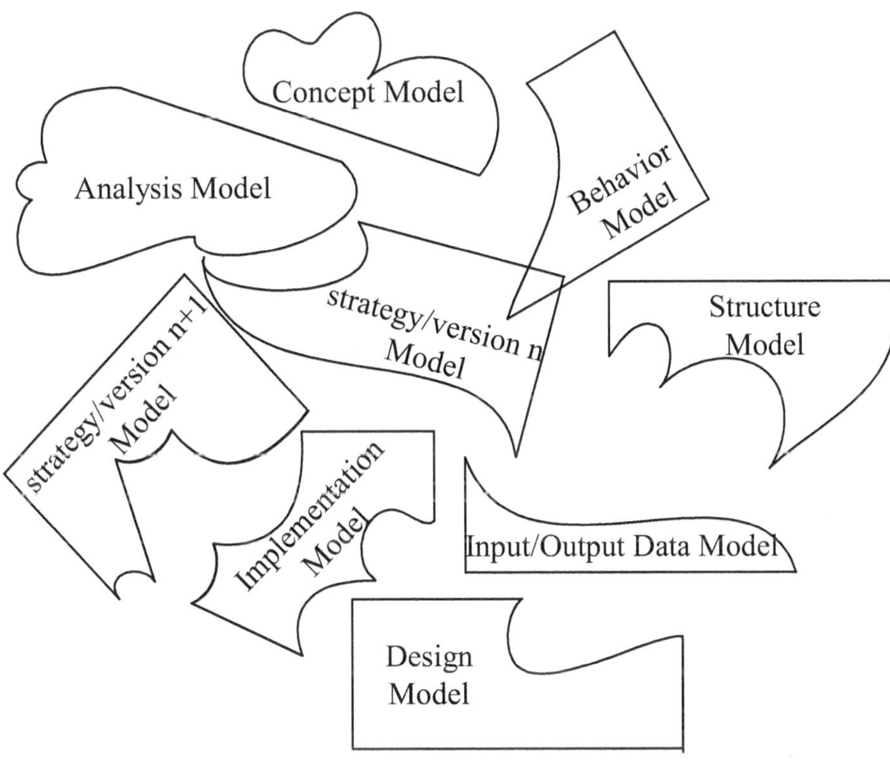

Figure 2-5. The Non-architectural Approach Picks a Model for Each View

The architectural approach, also known as the model singularity approach [Dori95, Dori02, Dori16, Pele02, Sode03], instead of picking many heterogeneous and separated models, will use only one single coalescence model as shown in Figure 2-6. The strategy/version n, strategy/version n+1, concept, analysis, design, implementation, structure, behavior and input/output data views are all integrated in this multiple views coalescence (MVC) model of software architecture (SA) [Chao14a, Chao14b, Chao14c, Chao15a, Chao15b, Chao16, Chao17a, Chao17b, Chao17c, Chao17d, Chao17e, Chao17f].

Figure 2-6. Software Architecture Uses a Coalescence Model

Figure 2-5 has many models. Figure 2-6 has only one model. Comparing Figure 2-5 with Figure 2-6, we unquestionably conclude that an integrated, holistic, united, coordinated, coherent and coalescence model is more favorable than a collection of many heterogeneous and separated models.

2-3 Definition of Software Architecture

Involved software systems are extremely complex in every aspect so that each stakeholder needs a blueprint or model to capture their essential structures and behaviors. Software architecture is such a blueprint or model.

There are several well-know definitions of software architecture [Burd10, Craw15, Dam06, Maie09, O'Rou03, Putm00, Roza11]. ANSI/IEEE 1471-2000 defines software architecture as: "the fundamental organization of a software system, embodied in its components, their relationships to each other and the environment, and the principles governing its design and evolution." The Open Group defines software architecture as either "a formal description of a system, or a detailed plan of the system at component level to guide its implementation," or as "the structure of components, their interrelationships, and the principles and guidelines governing their design and evolution over time" [Rayn09, Toga08].

Concluding the above definitions, we now give software architecture a definition of our own as shown in Figure 2-7.

> Software architecture is an integrated whole of a software system's multiple views, i.e., structure, behavior and other views, embodied in its assembled components, their interactions with each other and the environment, and the principles and guidelines governing its design and evolution.

Figure 2-7. Definition of Software Architecture

From the above definition, we find out that software architecture is an integrated whole of a system's multiple views, i.e., structure, behavior and other views, embodied in its assembled components, their interactions (or handshakes) with each other and the environment, and the principles and guidelines governing its design and evolution. That is, software architecture is an integrated and coalescence model of multiple views. In this coalescence model, structure, behavior and other views are all included in it as shown in Figure 2-8. We do not supply each view a respective model in this software architecture coalescence model.

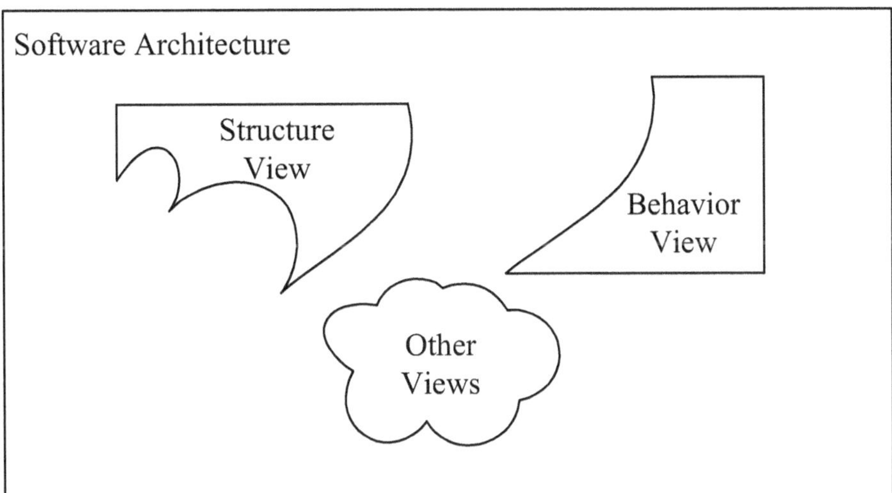

Figure 2-8. All Multiple Views are Included in This Software Architecture

Since multiple views are embodied in a software system's assembled components which belong to the structure view, they shall not exist alone. Multiple views must be loaded on the structure view just like a cargo is loaded on a ship as shown in Figure 2-9. There will be no multiple views if there is no structure view. Stand-alone multiple views are not meaningful.

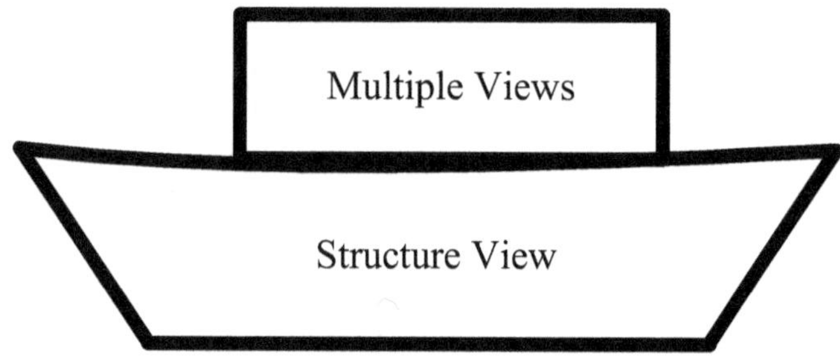

Figure 2-9. Multiple Views Must be Loaded on the Structure View

2-4 Architecture Description Language

An architecture description is a formal description and representation of a system. A description of the software architecture has to grasp the essence of the system and its details at the same time. In other words, an architecture description not only provides an overall picture that summarizes the whole system, but also contains enough detail that the system can be constructed and validated.

The language for architecture description is called the architecture description language (ADL) [Bass03, Clem02, Clem10, Dike01, Roza11, Shaw96, Tayl09]. An ADL is a special kind of language used in describing the architecture of a system.

Since the architectural approach uses a coalescence model for all multiple views of a system, the foremost duty of ADL is to make the strategy/version n, strategy/version n+1, concept, analysis, design, implementation, structure, behavior and input/output data views all integrated and coalesced within this architecture description.

2-5 Multiple Views Coalescence to Achieve the Software Architecture

Software architecture has been defined as a coalescence model of multiple views. Multiple views coalescence (MVC) uses only a single coalescence model as shown in Figure 2-10. Strategy/version n, strategy/version n+1, concept, analysis, design, implementation, structure, behavior and input/output data views are all integrated in this MVC architecture.

Figure 2-10. MVC Architecture

Generally, MVC architecture is synonymous with the software architecture. In other words, multiple views coalescence sets a path to achieve the software architecture as shown in Figure 2-11.

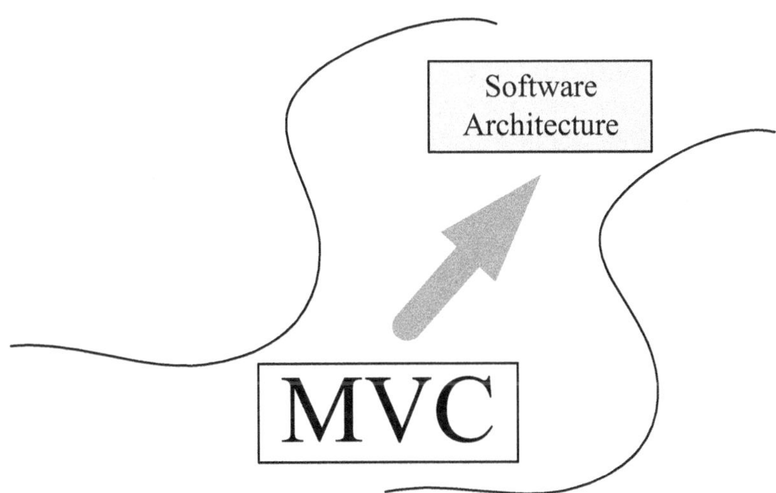

Figure 2-11. MVC to Achieve the Software Architecture

In the MVC architecture, multiple views must be attached to or built on the software structure. In other words, multiple views shall not exist alone; they must be loaded on the software structure just like a cargo is loaded on a ship as shown in

Figure 2-12. There will be no multiple views if there is no software structure. Stand-alone multiple views are not meaningful.

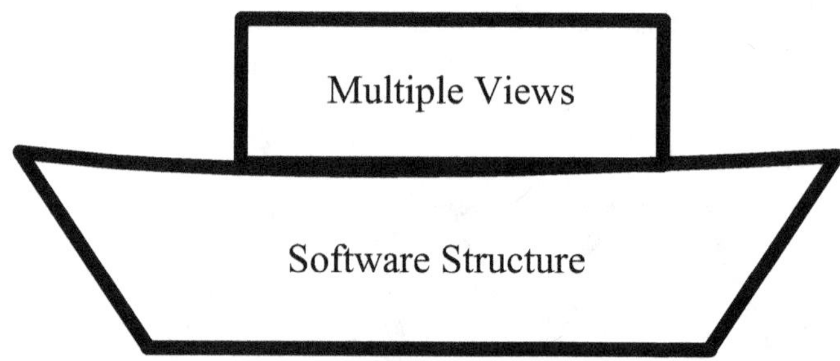

Figure 2-12. Multiple Views Must be Loaded on the Software Structure

2-6 Integrating the Software Structures and Software Behaviors

By integrating the software structure and software behavior, we obtain structure-behavior coalescence (SBC) within the system as shown in Figure 2-13.

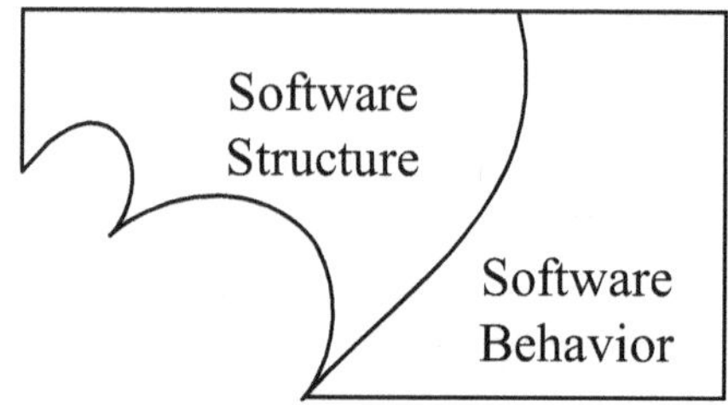

Figure 2-13. Structure-Behavior Coalescence

Structure-behavior coalescence has never been used in any systems model (SM) for software system development except the SBC architecture. There are many advantages to use the structure-behavior coalescence approach to integrate the software structure and software behavior.

SBC architecture uses a single model as shown in Figure 2-14. Software structures and software behaviors are integrated in this SBC architecture.

Figure 2-14. SBC Architecture

Since software structures and software behaviors are so tightly integrated, we sometimes claim that the core theme of SBC architecture is: Software Architecture = Software Structure + Software Behavior, as shown in Figure 2-15.

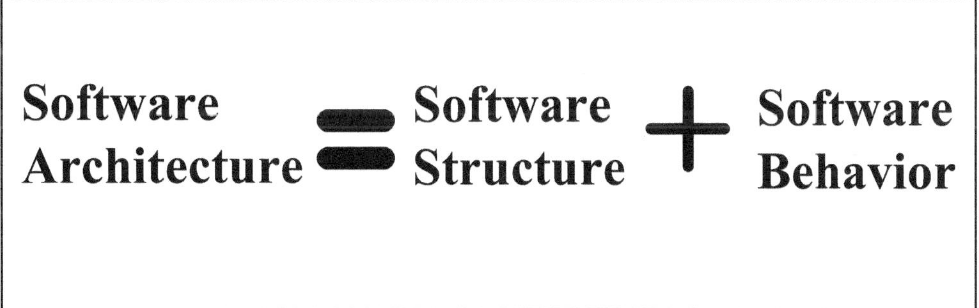

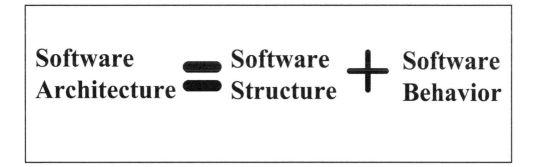

Figure 2-15. Core Theme of SBC Architecture

So far, software behaviors are separated from software structures in most cases [Pres09, Somm06]. For example, the well-known structured systems analysis and design (SSA&D) approach uses structure charts (SC) to represent the software structure and data flow diagrams (DFD) to represent the software behavior [Denn08, Kend10, Your99]. SC and DFD are two heterogeneous and separated models. They are so separated like that there is the "Antarctic Desert" between them, as shown in Figure 2-16.

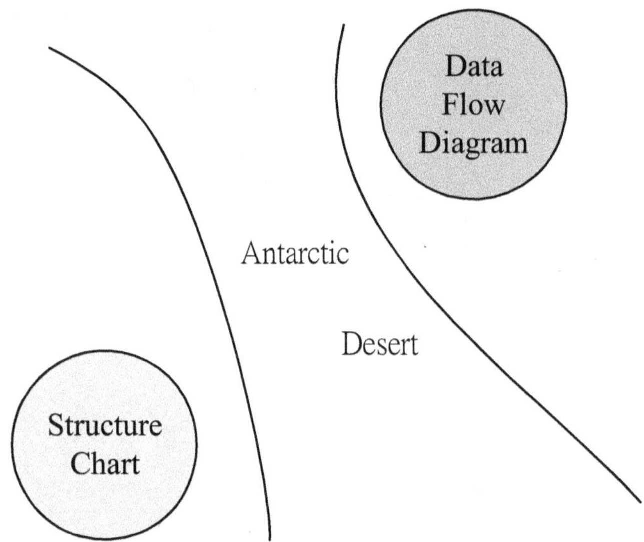

Figure 2-16. Two Heterogeneous and Separated Models

2-7 Structure-Behavior Coalescence to Facilitate Multiple Views Coalescence

Since structure and behavior views are the two most prominent ones among multiple views, integrating the structure and behavior views is clearly the best way to integrate multiple views of a software system. In other words, structure-behavior coalescence facilitates multiple views coalescence as shown in Figure 2-17.

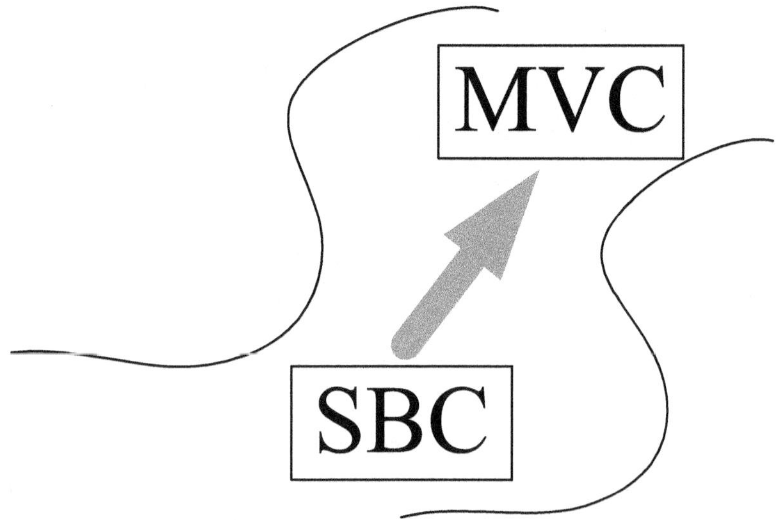

Figure 2-17. SBC Facilitates MVC

2-8 Structure-Behavior Coalescence to Achieve the Software Architecture

Figure 2-11 declares that multiple views coalescence sets a path to achieve the desired software architecture with the most efficient approach. Figure 2-17 declares that structure-behavior coalescence facilitates multiple views coalescence.

Combining the above two declarations, we conclude that structure-behavior coalescence sets a path to achieve the software architecture as shown in Figure 2-18. In this case, SBC architecture is also synonymous with the software architecture.

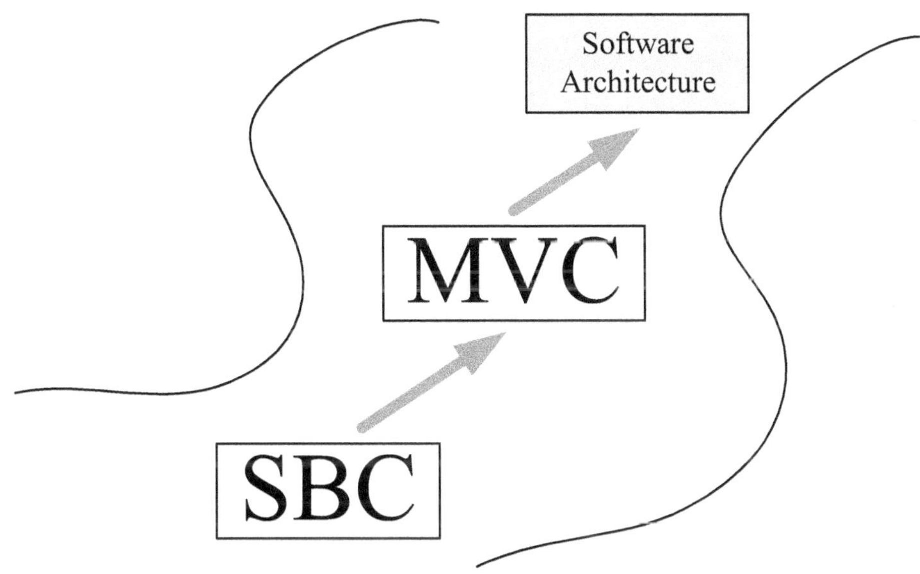

Figure 2-18. SBC to Achieve the Software Architecture

SBC architecture strongly demands that the structure and behavior views must be coalesced and integrated. This never happens in other architectural approaches such as Zachman Framework [O'Rou03], The Open Group Architecture Framework (TOGAF) [Rayn09, Toga08], Department of Defense Architecture Framework (DoDAF) [Dam06] and Unified Modeling Language (UML) [Rumb91]. Zachman Framework does not offer any mechanism to integrate the structure and behavior views. TOGAF, DoDAF and UML do not, either.

In the SBC architecture, the software behavior must be attached to or built on the software structure. In other words, the software behavior can not exist alone; it must be loaded on the software structure just like a cargo is loaded on a ship as shown in Figure 2-19. There will be no software behavior if there is no software structure. A stand-alone software behavior is not meaningful.

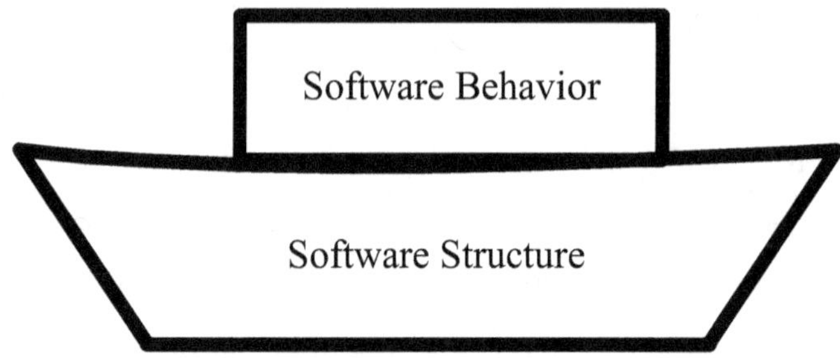

Figure 2-19. Software Behavior is Loaded on the Software Structure

2-9 Using SBC-ADL to Construct the Software Architecture

An architecture description language (ADL) is a special kind of language used in describing the architecture of a system [Shaw96, Tayl09].

A description of the software architecture has to grasp the essence of a system and its details at the same time. In other words, a software architecture description not only provides an overall picture that summarizes the system, but also contains enough detail that the system can be constructed and validated.

SBC-ADL uses six fundamental diagrams to describe the integration of software structure and software behavior of a system. These diagrams, as shown in Figure 2-20, are: a) architecture hierarchy diagram (AHD), b) framework diagram (FD), c) component operation diagram (COD), d) component connection diagram (CCD), e) structure-behavior coalescence diagram (SBCD) and f) interaction flow diagram (IFD).

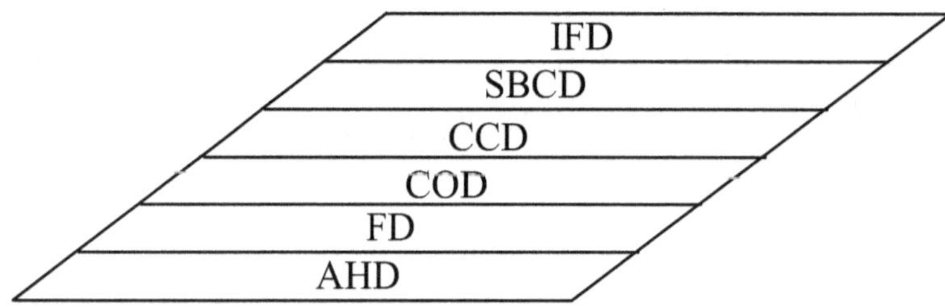

Figure 2-20. Six Fundamental Diagrams of SBC-ADL

SBC-ADL uses AHD, FD, COD, CCD, SBCD and IFD to depict the software structure and software behavior of a software system as shown in Figure 2-21.

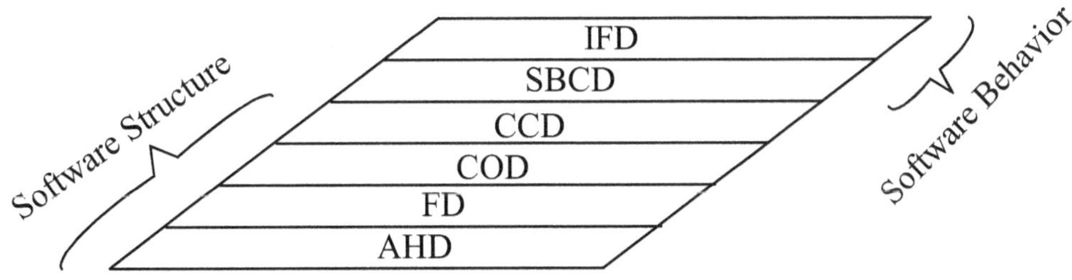

Figure 2-21. Software Structure and Software Behavior of a System

Examining the SBC-ADL approach, we find out that it depicts the software structure first and then depicts the software behavior later, not the other way around. The reason SBC-ADL does so lies in that the software behavior must be attached to or built on the software structure. With the software structure and attached software behavior, then, we can smoothly get the software architecture as shown in Figure 2-22.

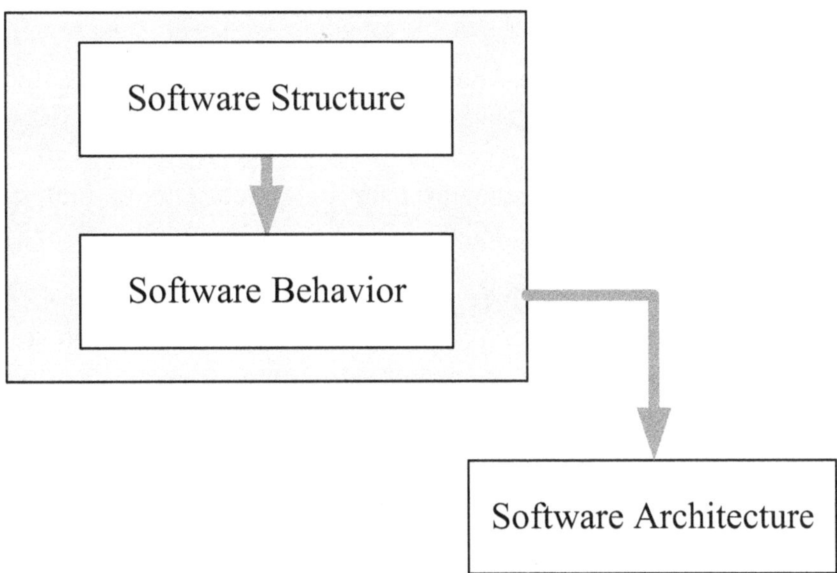

Figure 2-22. Software Behavior is Attached to the Software Structure

Let us ask the opposite question. Can the software structure be attached to or built on the software behavior? The answer is "No" as shown in Figure 2-23.

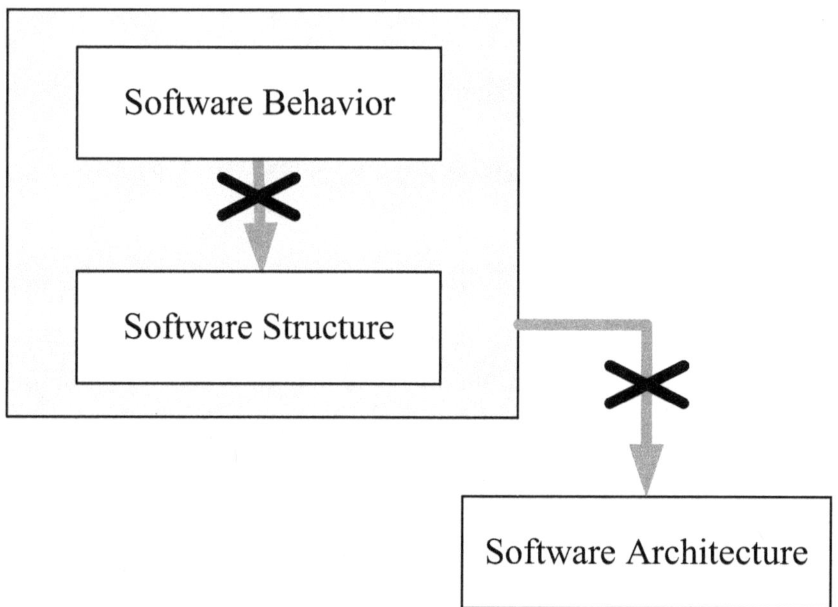

Figure 2-23. Software Structure is not Attached to the Software Behavior

In the SBC-ADL, software behavior must be attached to or built on the software structure. In other words, the software behavior shall not exist alone; it must be loaded on the software structure just like a cargo is loaded on a ship as shown in Figure 2-24. There will be no software behavior if there is no software structure. A stand-alone software behavior is not meaningful.

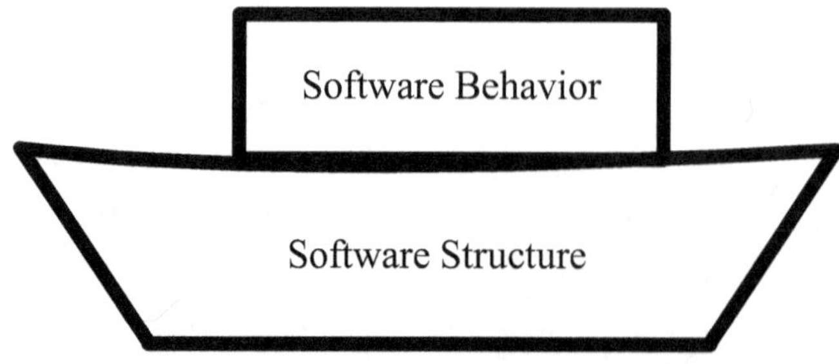

Figure 2-24. Software Behavior Must be Loaded on the Software Structure

AHD, FD, COD and CCD belong to software structure. SBCD and IFD belong to software behavior. Concluding the above discussion, we perceive that SBC-ADL will describe AHD, FD, COD and CCD first then describe SBCD and IFD later when it constructs the software architecture of a software system.

2-10 SBC Model Singularity

Channel-Based Single-Queue SBC Process Algebra (C-S-SBC-PA) [Chao17a], Channel-Based Multi-Queue SBC Process Algebra (C-M-SBC-PA) [Chao17b], Channel-Based Infinite-Queue SBC Process Algebra (C-I-SBC-PA) [Chao17c], Operation-Based Single-Queue SBC Process Algebra (O-S-SBC-PA) [Chao17d], Operation-Based Multi-Queue SBC Process Algebra (O-M-SBC-PA) [Chao17e] and Operation-Based Infinite-Queue SBC Process Algebra (O-I-SBC-PA) [Chao17f] are the six specialized SBC process algebras. The SBC process algebra (SBC-PA) shown in Figure 2-25 is a model singularity approach.

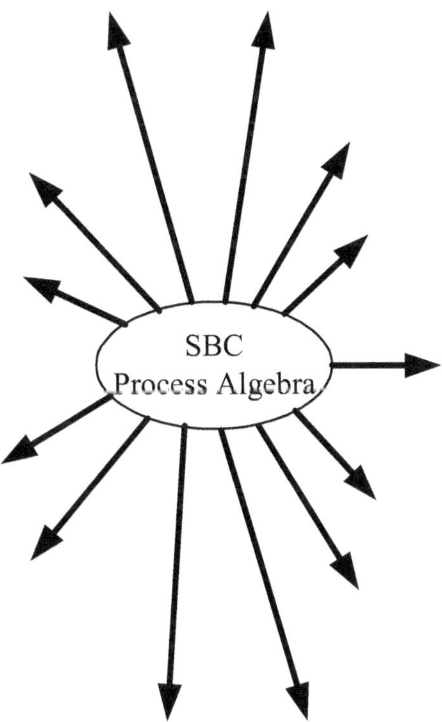

Figure 2-25. SBC-PA is a Model Singularity Approach.

The SBC architecture description language (SBC-ADL) is also a model singularity approach. With SBC mind set sitting in the kernel, the SBC-ADL single model shown in Figure 2-26 is therefore able to represent all structural views such as architecture hierarchy diagram (AHD), framework diagram (FD), component operation diagram (COD), component connection diagram (CCD) and behavioral views such as structure-behavior coalescence diagram (SBCD), interaction flow diagram (IFD).

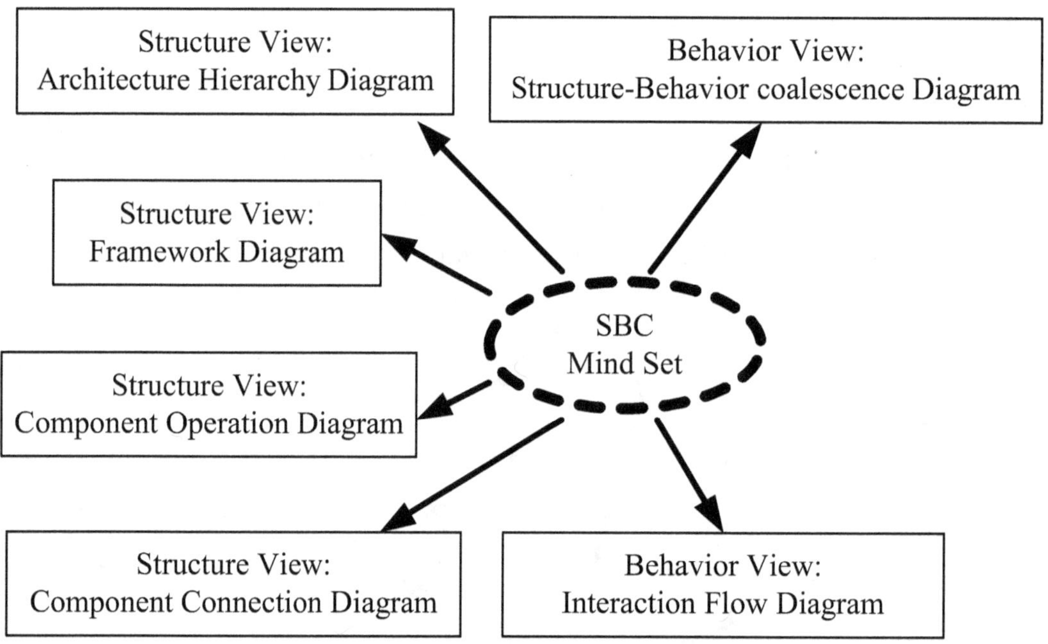

Figure 2-26. SBC-ADL is a Model Singularity Approach.

The combination of SBC process algebra (SBC-PA) and SBC architecture description language (SBC-ADL) is shown in Figure 2-27, again as a model singularity approach.

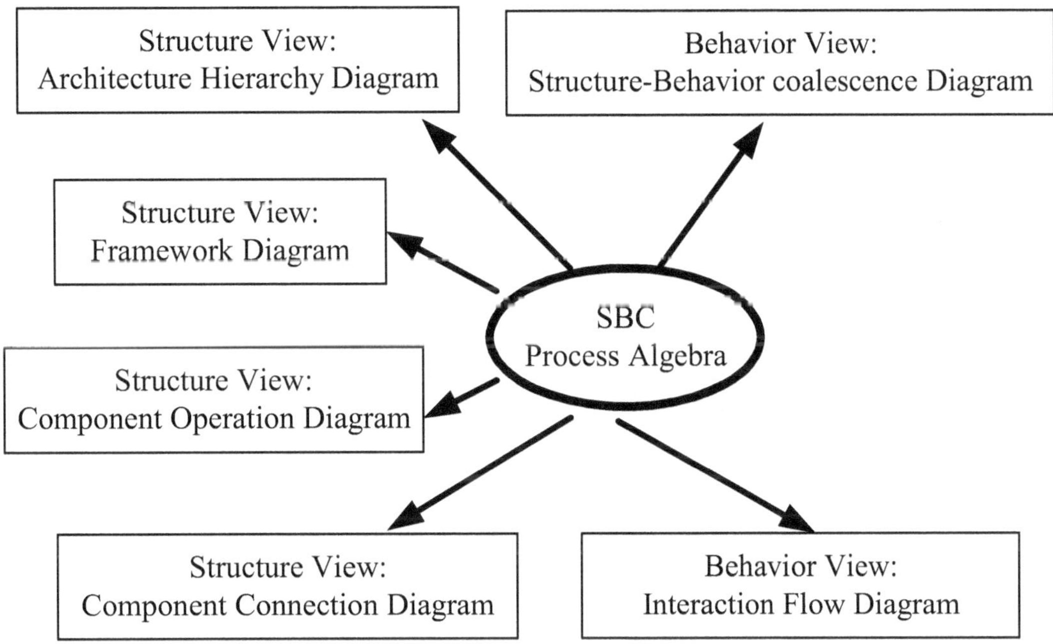

Figure 2-27. SBC Model is a Model Singularity Approach.

PART II: SBC ARCHITECTURE DESCRIPTION LANGUAGE

Chapter 3: Software Structure

SBC-ADL uses the architecture hierarchy diagram, framework diagram, component operation diagram and component connection diagram to depict the software structure of a software system.

3-1 Architecture Hierarchy Diagram

Software architects use an architecture hierarchy diagram (AHD) to define the multi-level (hierarchical) decomposition and composition of a software system. AHD is the first fundamental diagram to achieve structure-behavior coalescence.

3-1-1 Decomposition and Composition

The following is an example of systems decomposition and composition. The *Computer* system consists of *Monitor*, *Keyboard*, *Mouse* and *Case*, as shown in Figure 3-1. The *Monitor*, *Keyboard*, *Mouse* and *Case* are subsystems comprising the *Computer* system.

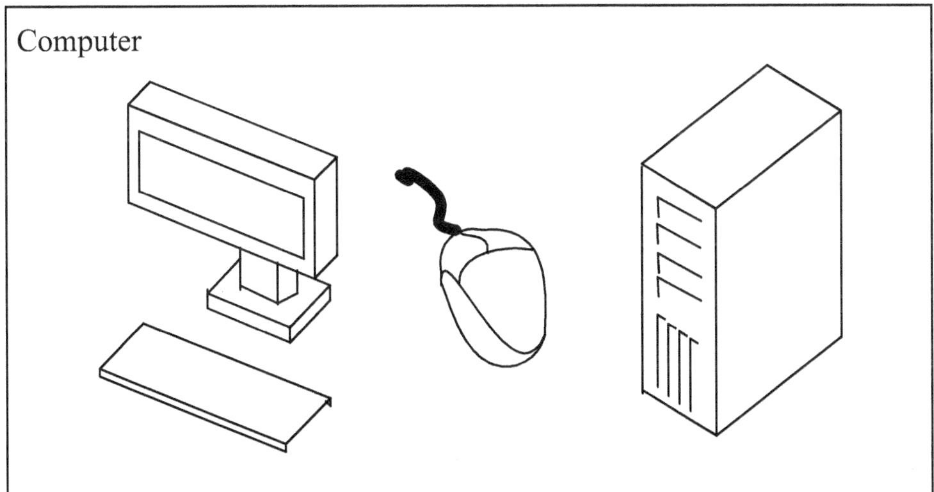

Figure 3-1. Decomposition and Composition of the *Computer* System

Another example indicates that the *Tree* system is composed of *Root* and *Stem*, as shown in Figure 3-2. In this example, we would say that the *Root* and *Stem* are subsystems, respectively, while the *Tree* system consists of its subsystems.

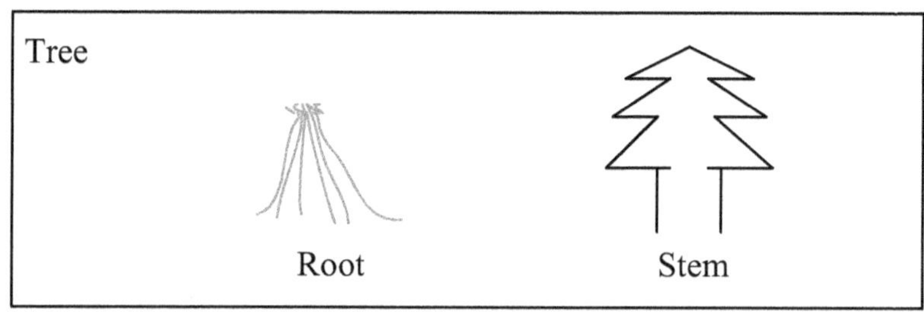

Figure 3-2. Decomposition and Composition of the *Tree* System

The last example demonstrates that the *SBC_Book* system is composed of *Chapter_1*, *Part_1* and *Part_2*, as shown in Figure 3-3. In this example, we would say that *Chapter_1*, *Part_1* and *Part_2* are subsystems, respectively while the *SBC_Book* system consists of its subsystems.

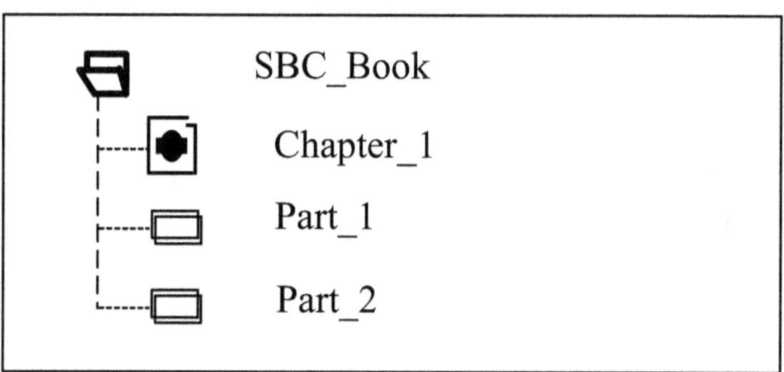

Figure 3-3. Decomposition and Composition of the *SBC_Book* System

Architecture hierarchy diagram (AHD) is used to define the decomposition and composition of a system. As an example, Figure 3-4 shows an AHD of the *Computer* system. We clearly observe that the *Computer* system is composed of *Monitor*, *Keyboard*, *Mouse* and *Case*.

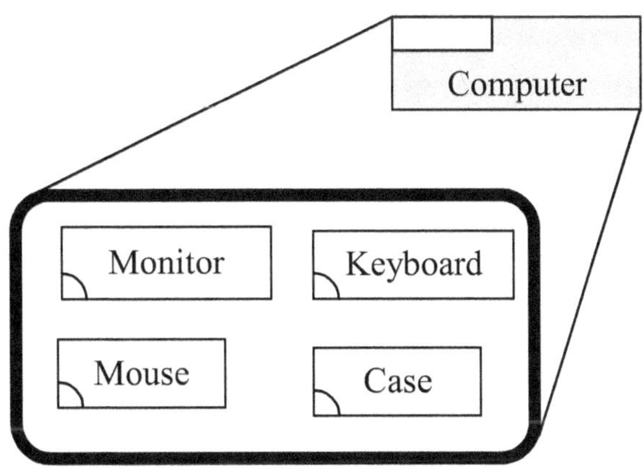

Figure 3-4. AHD of the *Computer* System

As a second example, Figure 3-5 shows an AHD of the *Tree* system. We clearly observe that the *Tree* system is composed of *Root* and *Stem*.

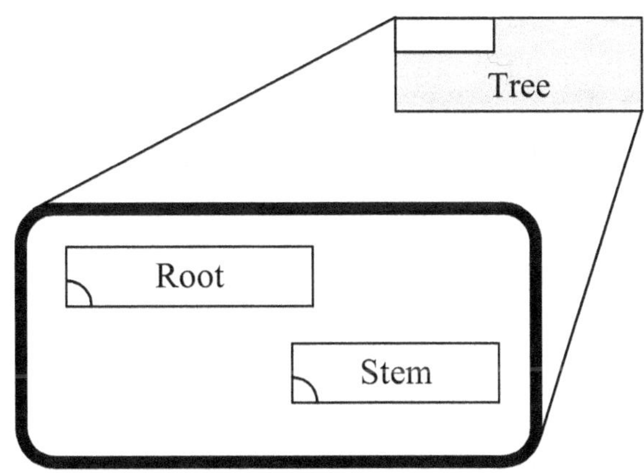

Figure 3-5. AHD of the *Tree* System

As a third example, Figure 3-6 shows an AHD of the *SBC_Book* system. We clearly observe that the *SBC_Book* is composed of *Chapter_1*, *Part_1* and *Part_2*.

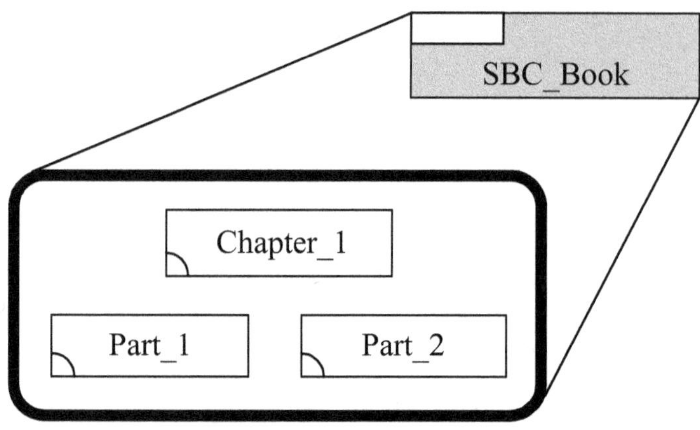

Figure 3-6. AHD of the *SBC_Book* system

3-1-2 Multi-Level Decomposition and Composition

The subsystem may also contain subsystems as we further decompose it. For example, *Case* is a subsystem of the *Computer*, and we can further decompose it into *Motherboard*, *Hard_Disk*, *Power_Supply* and *DVD_Disk*, as shown in Figure 3-7.

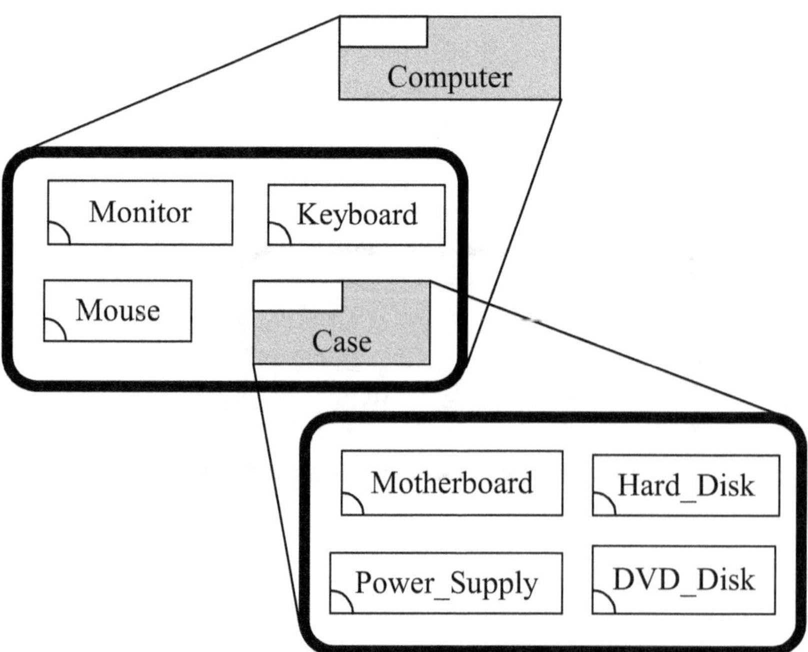

Figure 3-7. Multi-Level Decomposition/Composition of the *Computer* System

As a second example, *Stem* is a subsystem of the *Tree*, and we can further decompose it into *Trunk* and *Leaf*, as shown in Figure 3-8.

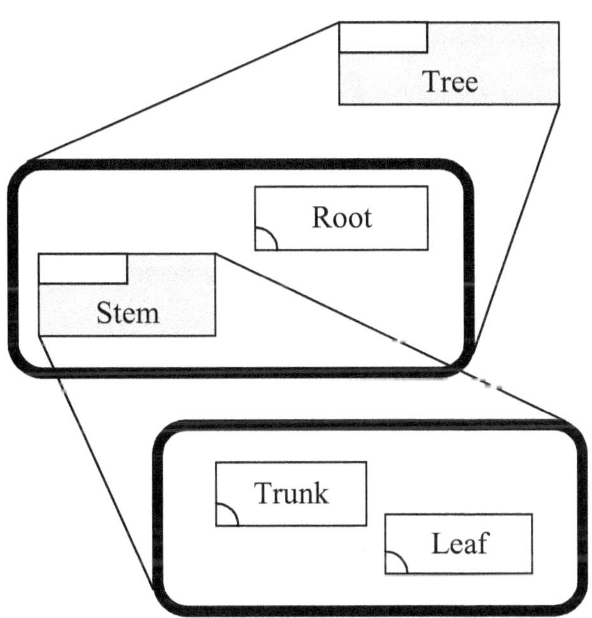

Figure 3-8. Multi-Level Decomposition/Composition of the *Tree* System

As a third example, *Part_1* is a subsystem of the *SBC_Book*, and we can further decompose it into *Chapter_2* and *Chapter_3*; *Part_2* is also a subsystem of the *SBC_Book*, and we can further decompose it into *Chapter_4* and *Chapter_5*, as shown in Figure 3-9.

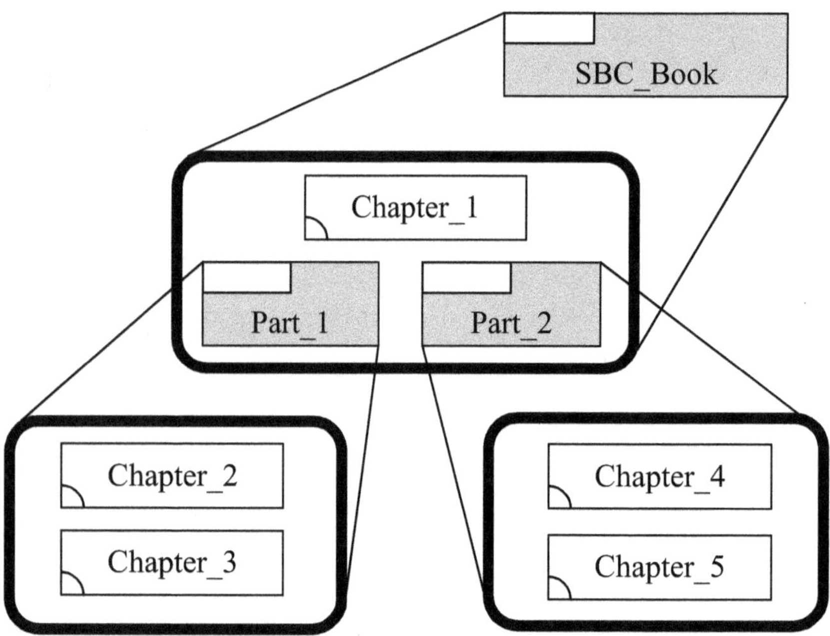

Figure 3-9. Multi-Level Decomposition/Composition of the *SBC_Book* System

Generally speaking, multi-level decomposition and composition of a system is applied often in constructing its architecture. To make a complex system look simple, the mechanism of multi-level composition and decomposition should always be used.

3-1-3 Aggregated and Non-Aggregated Systems

Any subsystem (at any level) involved with multi-level decomposition and composition of a system is either aggregated or non-aggregated. The definition of aggregated and non-aggregated systems is shown in Figure 3-10.

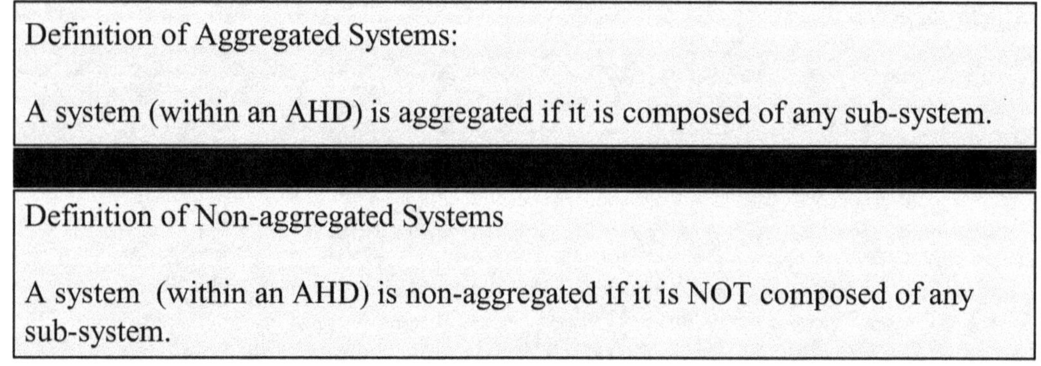

Definition of Aggregated Systems:

A system (within an AHD) is aggregated if it is composed of any sub-system.

Definition of Non-aggregated Systems

A system (within an AHD) is non-aggregated if it is NOT composed of any sub-system.

Figure 3-10. Definition of Aggregated and Non-aggregated Systems

Non-aggregated systems are sometimes referred to as components, parts, entities, objects and building blocks [Chao14a, Chao14b, Chao14c].

In the multi-level systems decomposition and composition, any system is either aggregated or non-aggregated, but not both. For example, in Figure 3-4, *Case* is a non-aggregated system, not an aggregated system. As an interesting contrast, in Figure 3-7, *Case* is an aggregated system, not a non-aggregated system.

As a second example, in Figure 3-5, *Stem* is a non-aggregated system, not an aggregated system. As an interesting contrast, in Figure 3-8, *Stem* is an aggregated system, not a non-aggregated system.

As a third example, in Figure 3-6, *Part_1 and Part_2* are non-aggregated systems, not aggregated systems. As an interesting contrast, in Figure 3-9, *Part_1* and *Part_2* are aggregated systems, not non-aggregated systems.

3-2 Framework Diagram

Framework diagram (FD) enables software architects to examine the multi-layer (also referred to as multi-tier) decomposition and composition of a system. FD is the second fundamental diagram to achieve structure-behavior coalescence.

3-2-1 Multi-Layer Decomposition and Composition

Decomposition and composition of a system can also be represented in a multi-layer (or multi-tier) manner. We draw a framework diagram (FD) for the multi-layer decomposition and composition of a system.

As an example, Figure 3-11 shows a FD of the *Computer* system. In the figure, *Technology_SubLayer_2* contains *Monitor*, *Keyboard* and *Mouse*; *Technology_SubLayer_1* contains *Motherboard*, *Hard_Disk*, *Power_Supply* and *DVD_Disk*.

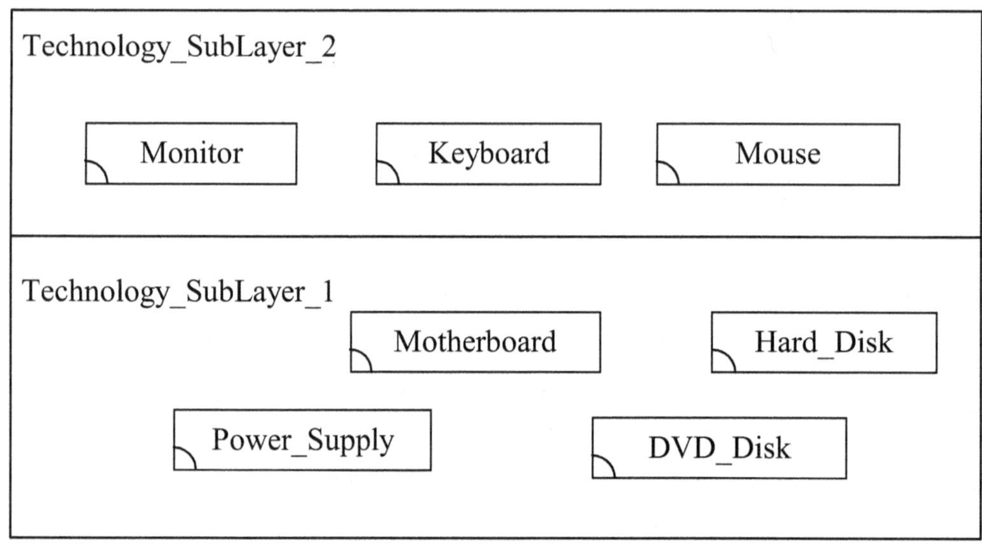

Figure 3-11. FD of the *Computer* System

As a second example, Figure 3-12 shows a FD of the *Tree* system. In the figure, *Technology_SubLayer_2* contains *Root*; *Technology_SubLayer_1* contains *Trunk* and *Leaf*.

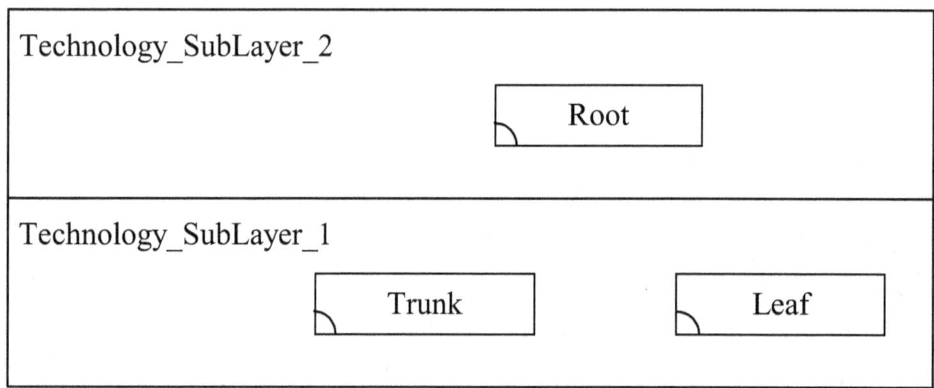

Figure 3-12. FD of the *Tree* System

As a third example, Figure 3-13 shows a FD of the *SBC_Book* system. In the figure, *Technology_SubLayer_2* contains *Chapter_1*; *Technology_SubLayer_1* contains *Chapter_2*, *Chapter_3*, *Chapter_4* and *Chapter_5*.

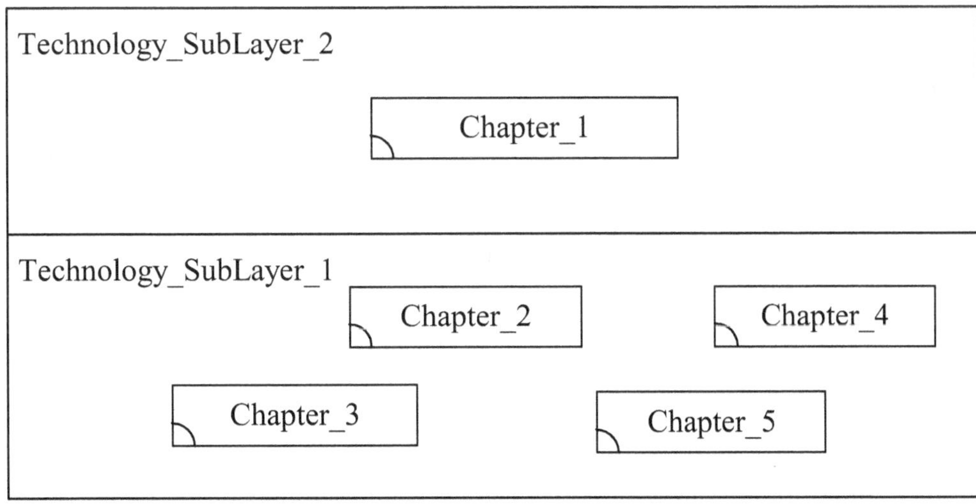

Figure 3-13. FD of the *SBC_Book* System

3-2-2 Only Non-Aggregated Systems Appearing in Framework Diagrams

Both aggregated and non-aggregated systems are displayed in the multi-level AHD decomposition and composition of a system. As an interesting contrast, only non-aggregated systems shall appear in the multi-layer FD decomposition and composition of a system.

For example, Figure 3-7 in the previous section shows an AHD of the *Computer* system in which both aggregated systems such as *Computer*, *Case* and non-aggregated systems such as *Monitor*, *Keyboard*, *Mouse*, *Motherboard*, *Hard_Disk*, *Power_Supply*, *DVD_Disk* are displayed. As an interesting contrast, Figure 3-11 in the previous section shows a FD of the *Computer* system in which only non-aggregated systems such as *Monitor*, *Keyboard*, *Mouse*, *Motherboard*, *Hard_Disk*, *Power_Supply* and *DVD_Disk* are displayed.

For a second example, Figure 3-8 in the previous section shows an AHD of the *Tree* system in which both aggregated systems such as *Tree*, *Stem* and non-aggregated systems such as *Root*, *Trunk*, *Leaf* are displayed. As an interesting contrast, Figure 3-12 in the previous section shows a FD of the *Tree* system in which only non-aggregated systems such as *Root*, *Trunk* and *Leaf* are displayed.

For a third example, Figure 3-9 in the previous section shows an AHD of the *SBC_Book* system in which both aggregated systems such as *SBC_Book*, *Part_1*, *Part_2* and non-aggregated systems such as *Chapter_1*, *Chapter_2*, *Chapter_3*, *Chapter_4*, *Chapter_5* are displayed. As an interesting contrast, Figure 3-13 in the previous section shows a FD of the *SBC_Book* system in which only non-aggregated systems such as *Chapter_1*, *Chapter_2*, *Chapter_3*, *Chapter_4* and *Chapter_5* are displayed.

3-3 Component Operation Diagram

Software architects use a component operation diagram (COD) to display all components' operations of a system. COD is the third fundamental diagram to achieve structure-behavior coalescence.

3-3-1 Operations of Components

An operation provided by each component represents a procedure, or method, or function of the component. If other systems request this component to perform an operation, then shall use it to accomplish the operation request.

Each component in a software system must possess at least one operation. A component should not exist in a system if it does not possess any operation. Figure 3-14 shows that component *SalePurchase_UI* has four operations: *SaleInputClick*, *SalePrintClick*, *PurchaseInputClick* and *PurchasePrintClick*.

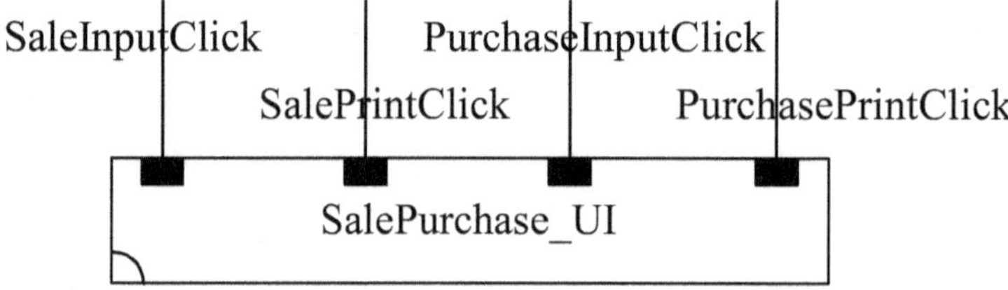

Figure 3-14. Four Operations of the *SalePurchase_UI* Component

An operation formula is utilized to fully represent an operation. An operation formula includes a) operation name, b) input parameters and c) output parameters as shown in Figure 3-15.

$$\text{Operation\_Name (In } i_1, i_2, ..., i_m \text{ ; Out } o_1 , o_2, ..., o_n \text{)}$$

Figure 3-15. Operation Formula

Operation name is the name of this operation. In a system, every operation name should be unique. Duplicate operation names shall not be allowed in any system.

An operation may have several input and output parameters. The input and output parameters, gathered from all operations, represent the input data and output data views of a system [Date03, Elma10]. As shown in Figure 3-16, component *SalePrint_UI* possesses the *ShowModal* operation which has no input/output parameter; component *SalePrint_UI* also possesses the *SalePrintButtonClick* operation which has the *sDate* and *sNo* input parameters (with the arrow direction pointing to the component) and the *s_report* output parameter (with the arrow direction opposite to the component).

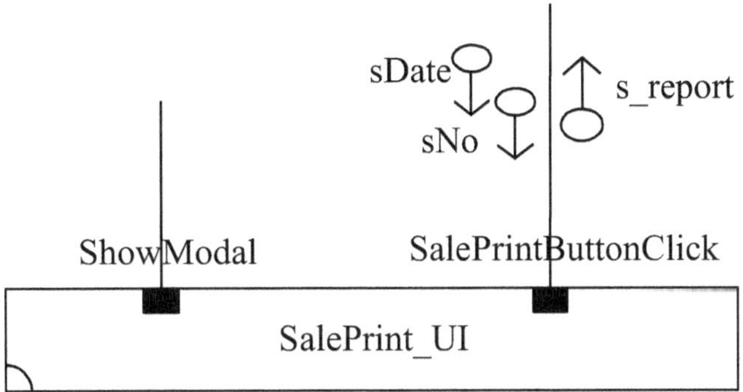

Figure 3-16. Input/Output Parameters of *SalePrintButtonClick*

Data formats of input and output parameters can be described by data type specifications. There are two sets of data types: primitive and composite [Date03, Elma10]. Figure 3-17 shows the primitive data type specification of the *sDate* and *sNo* input parameters occurring in the *SalePrintButtonClick(In sDate, sNo; Out s_report)* operation formula.

Parameter	Data Type	Instances
sDate	Text	20100517, 20100612
sNo	Text	001, 002

Figure 3-17. Primitive Data Type Specification

Figure 3-18 shows the composite data type specification of the *s_report* output parameter occurring in the *SalePrintButtonClick(In sDate, sNo; Out s_report)* operation formula.

<table>
<tr><td>Parameter</td><td>s_report</td></tr>
<tr><td>Data Type</td><td>TABLE of
Sale Date : Text
Sale No : Text
Customer : Text
ProductNo : Text
Quantity : Integer
UnitPrice : Real
Total : Real
End TABLE;</td></tr>
<tr><td>Instances</td><td>Sale Date : 20100517 Sale No : 001
Customer : Larry Fink
<table><tr><td>ProductNo</td><td>Quantity</td><td>UnitPrice</td></tr><tr><td>A12345</td><td>400</td><td>100.00</td></tr><tr><td>A00001</td><td>300</td><td>200.00</td></tr></table>Total : 100,000.00</td></tr>
</table>

Figure 3-18. Composite Data Type Specification

3-3-2 Drawing the Component Operation Diagram

For a system, COD is used to display all components' operations. Figure 3-19 shows the *Multi-Tier Personal Data System's COD*. In the figure, component *MTPDS_UI* has two operations: *Calculate_AgeClick* and *Calculate_OverweightClick*; component *Age_Logic* has one operation: *Calculate_Age*; component *Overweight_Logic* has one operation: *Calculate_Overweight*; component *Personal_Database* has two operations: *Sql_DateOfBirth_Select* and *Sql_SexHeightWeight_Select*.

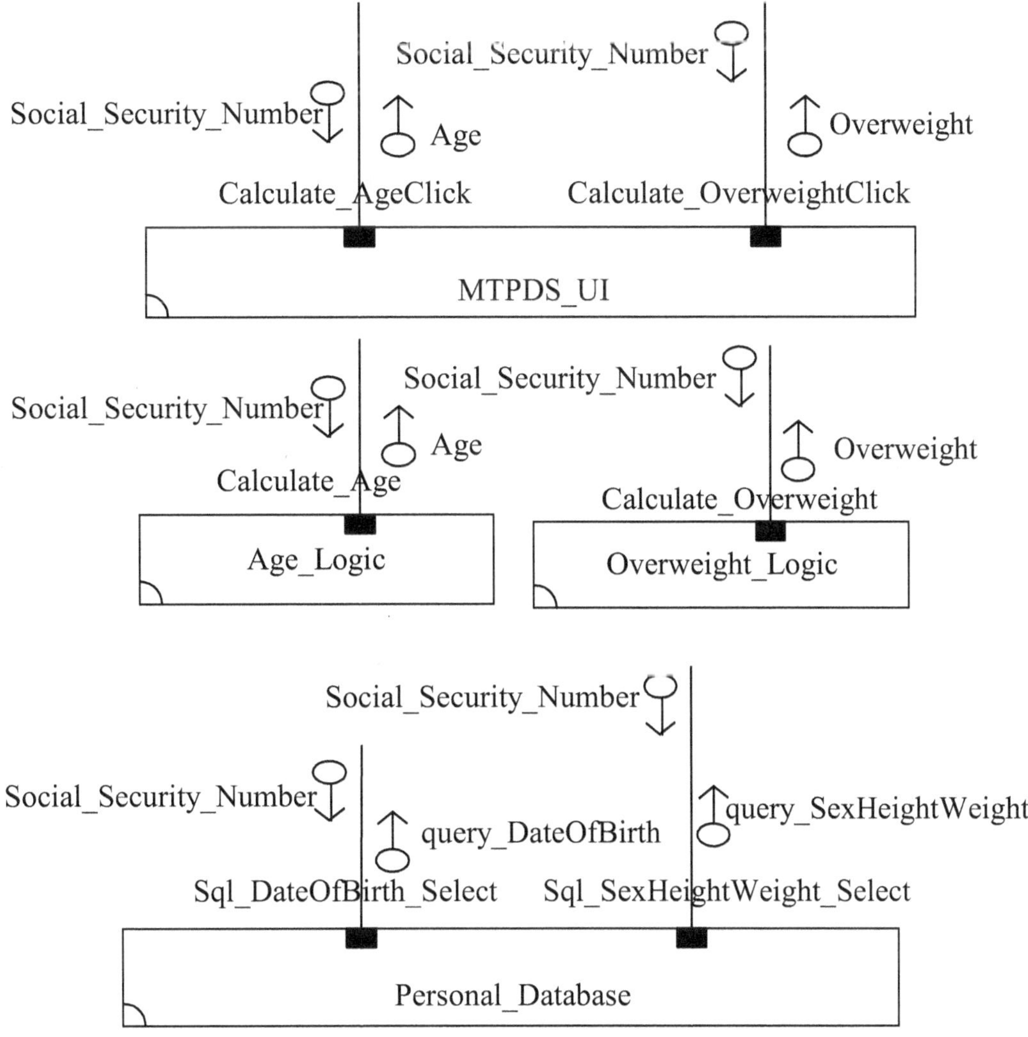

Figure 3-19. COD of the *Multi-Tier Personal Data System*

The operation formula of *Calculate_AgeClick* is *Calculate_AgeClick(In Social_Security_Number; Out Age)*. The operation formula of *Calculate_OverweightClick* is *Calculate_OverweightClick(In Social_Security_Number; Out Overweight)*. The operation formula of *Calculate_Age* is *Calculate_Age(In Social_Security_Number; Out Age)*. The operation formula of *Calculate_Overweight* is *Calculate_Overweight(In Social_Security_Number; Out Overweight)*. The operation formula of *Sql_DateOfBirth_Select* is *Sql_DateOfBirth_Select(In Social_Security_Number; Out query_DateOfBirth)*. The operation formula of *Sql_SexHeightWeight_Select* is *Sql_SexHeightWeight_Select(In Social_Security_Number; Out query_SexHeightWeight)*.

Figure 3-20 shows the primitive data type specification of the *Social_Security_Number* input parameter and the *Age*, *Overweight* output parameters.

Parameter	Data Type	Instances
Social_Security_Number	Text	424-87-3651, 512-24-3722
Age	Integer	28, 56
Overweight	Boolean	Yes, No

Figure 3-20. Primitive Data Type Specification

Figure 3-21 shows the composite data type specification of the *query_DateOfBirth* output parameter occurring in the *Sql_DateOfBirth_Select(In Social_Security_Number; Out query_DateOfBirth)* operation formula.

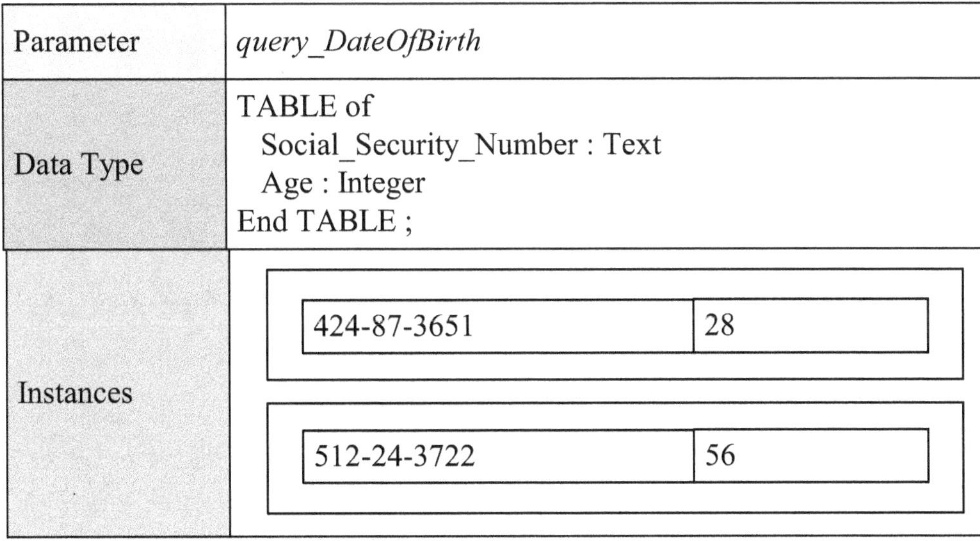

Parameter	*query_DateOfBirth*
Data Type	TABLE of Social_Security_Number : Text Age : Integer End TABLE ;
Instances	424-87-3651 | 28 512-24-3722 | 56

Figure 3-21. Composite Data Type Specification

Figure 3-22 shows the composite data type specification of the *query_SexHeightWeight* output parameter occurring in the *Sql_SexHeightWeight_Select(In Social_Security_Number; Out query_SexHeightWeight)* operation formula.

Parameter	*query_SexHeightWeight*
Data Type	TABLE of Social_Security_Number : Text Sex : Text Height : Number Weight : Number End TABLE ;
Instances	424-87-3651 | Female | 162 | 76 512-24-3722 | Male | 180 | 80

Figure 3-22. Composite Data Type Specification

3-4 Component Connection Diagram

A component connection diagram (CCD) is utilized to describe how all components and actors are connected within a system. CCD is the fourth fundamental diagram to achieve structure-behavior coalescence.

3-4-1 Essence of a Connection

A connection implies an operation request. When an operation is used by another subsystem then a connection appears. Accordingly, a connection is defined as the linkage that is constructed when an operation is used by another subsystem. Figure 3-23 shows that Subs*ystem_A* uses the *Salary_Calculation* operation provided by the *Component_B* component.

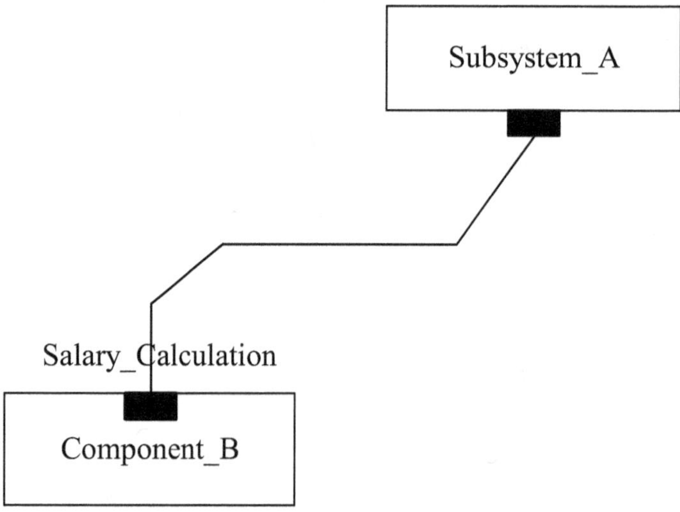

Figure 3-23. A Connection Appears When an Operation is Used

The above figure describes, sufficiently, the essence of a connection. However, we seldom use this kind of drawing. Instead, a simplified drawing of the above figure is often used as shown in Figure 3-24.

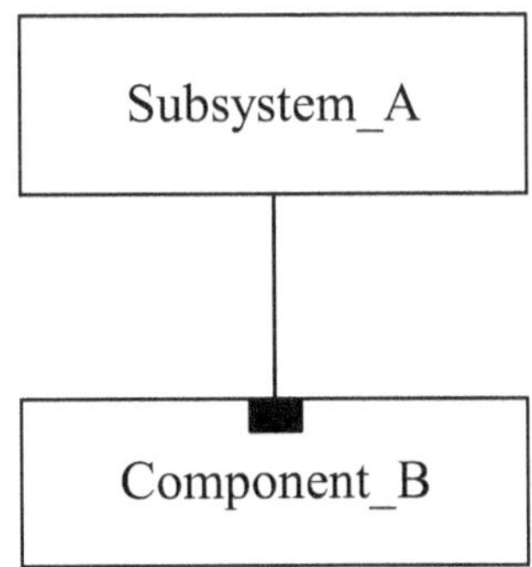

Figure 3-24. Simplified Drawing of a Connection

Since an operation is always provided by a component, there is no doubt that the *Component_B* operation provider is a component. On the contrary, the *Subsystem_A* operation user can be either a component (e.g., *Component_A*) or an actor (e.g., *Actor_A*) as shown in Figure 3-25. An actor belongs to the external environment of a system.

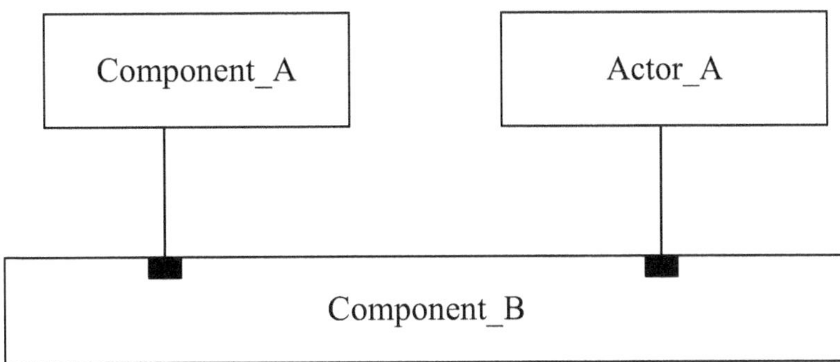

Figure 3-25. Operation User is Either a Component Or an Actor

Within a connection the subsystem (either a component or an actor) using the operation is always entitled the *Client* and the component which provides the operation is always entitled the *Server* as Figure 3-26 shows.

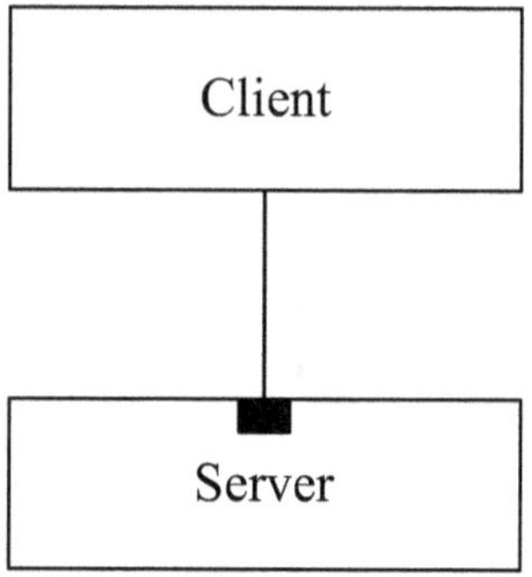

Figure 3-26. Roles of Client and Server Within a Connection

3-4-2 Drawing the Component Connection Diagram

A component connection diagram (CCD) is utilized to describe how all components and actors (in the external environment) are connected within a system. Figure 3-27 exhibits the *Multi-Tier Personal Data System's* COD.

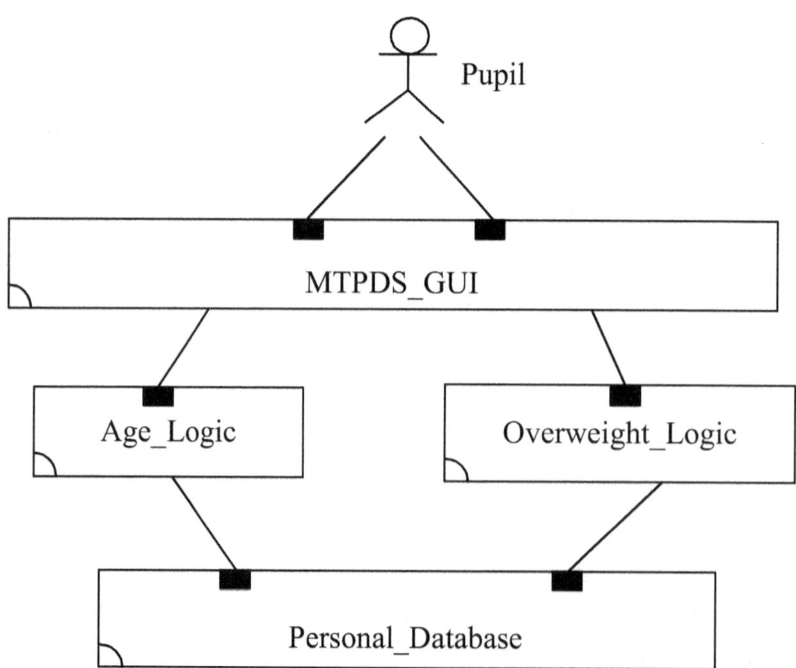

Figure 3-27. CCD of the *Multi-Tier Personal Data System*

In Figure 3-27, actor *Pupil* has two connections with the *MTPDS_UI* component; component *MTPDS_UI* has one connection with each of the *Age_Logic* and *Overweight_Logic* components; component *Age_Logic* has a connection with the *Personal_Database* component; component *Overweight_Logic* has a connection with the *Personal_Database* component.

After finishing the CCD, the formation pattern of the *Multi-Tier Personal Data System* will be constructed; thus the software structure of the *Multi-Tier Personal Data System* becomes more transparent.

Chapter 4: Software Behavior

SBC-ADL uses the structure-behavior coalescence diagram and interaction flow diagram to delineate the software behavior of a system.

4-1 Structure-Behavior Coalescence Diagram

Structure-behavior coalescence diagram (SBCD) enables a system architect to observe the structure and behavior coexisting in a system. SBCD is the fifth fundamental diagram to achieve structure-behavior coalescence.

4-1-1 Purpose of Structure-Behavior Coalescence Diagram

The major aim of the SBC-ADL approach is to achieve the integration of software structure and software behavior within a system. SBCD enables a system architect to observe the software structure and software behavior coexisting in a system. This is the purpose of utilizing SBCD when architecting the software architecture.

Figure 4-1 exhibits the *Multi-Tier Personal Data System*'s SBCD In this example, interactions among the *Pupil* actor and the *MTPDS_UI*, *Age_Logic*, *Overweight_Logic* and *Personal_Database* components shall draw forth the *AgeCalculation* and *OverweightCalculation* behaviors.

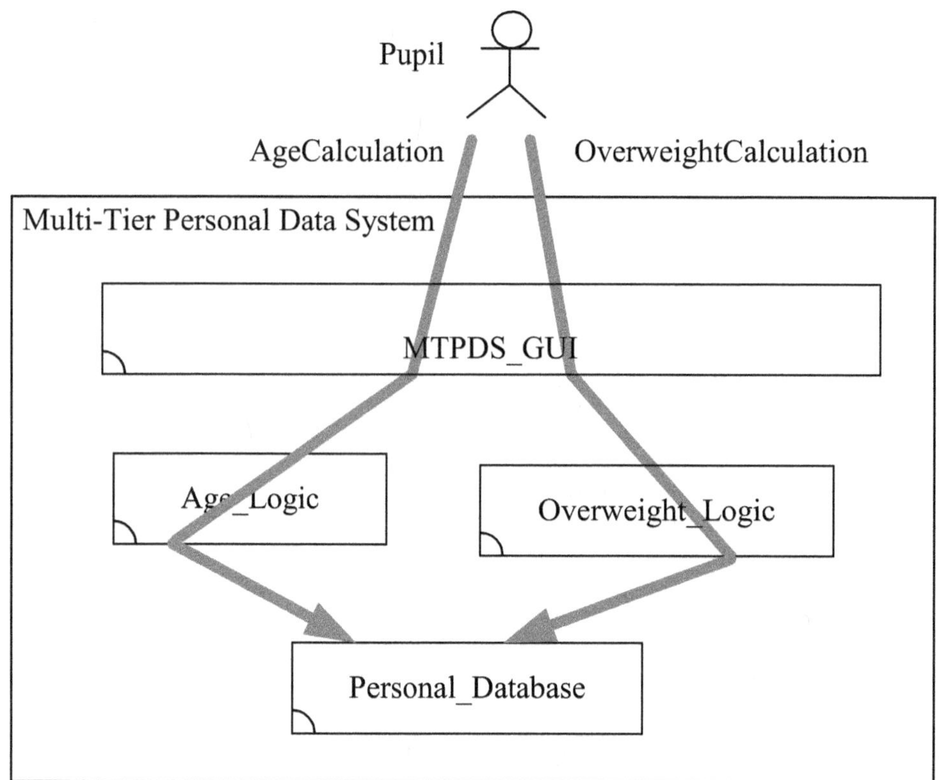

Figure 4-1. SBCD of the *Multi-Tier Personal Data System*

The overall behavior of a system is the aggregation of all its individual behaviors. All individual behaviors are mutually independent of each other. They tend to be executed concurrently [Hoar85, Miln89, Miln99]. For example, the overall behavior of the *Multi-Tier Personal Data System* includes the *AgeCalculation* and *OverweightCalculation* behaviors. In other words, the *AgeCalculation* and *OverweightCalculation* behaviors are combined to produce the overall behavior of the *Multi-Tier Personal Data System*.

The major purpose of using the architectural approach, instead of separating the structure model from the behavior model, is to achieve a coalesced model. In Figure 4-1, software architects are able to see the software structure and software behavior coexisting in a SBCD. That is, in the *Multi-Tier Personal Data System's* SBCD, we not only see its software structure but also see (at the same time) its software behavior.

4-1-2 Drawing the Structure-Behavior Coalescence Diagram

Let us now explain the usage of SBCD by constructing a SBCD step by step. The goal of having a SBCD is enabling software architects to see both the structure and behavior, simultaneously. In order to achieve this goal, a SBCD is drawn by first constructing all of the components, then describing the external environment's actors, and finally describing the interactions among these components and the external environment's actors.

For example, the *Multi-Tier Personal Data System* has two behaviors: *AgeCalculation* and *OverweightCalculation*. After constructing the *Multi-Tier Personal Data System* with all its components, the external environment's actors and the *AgeCalculation* behavior, we obtain the graphical representation as shown in Figure 4-2. In this Figure, the *AgeCalculation* behavior indicates that actor *Pupil* interacts with the *MTPDS_UI* component first, then component *MTPDS_UI* interacts with the *Age_Logic* component later, then component *Age_Logic* interacts with the *Personal_Database* component finally.

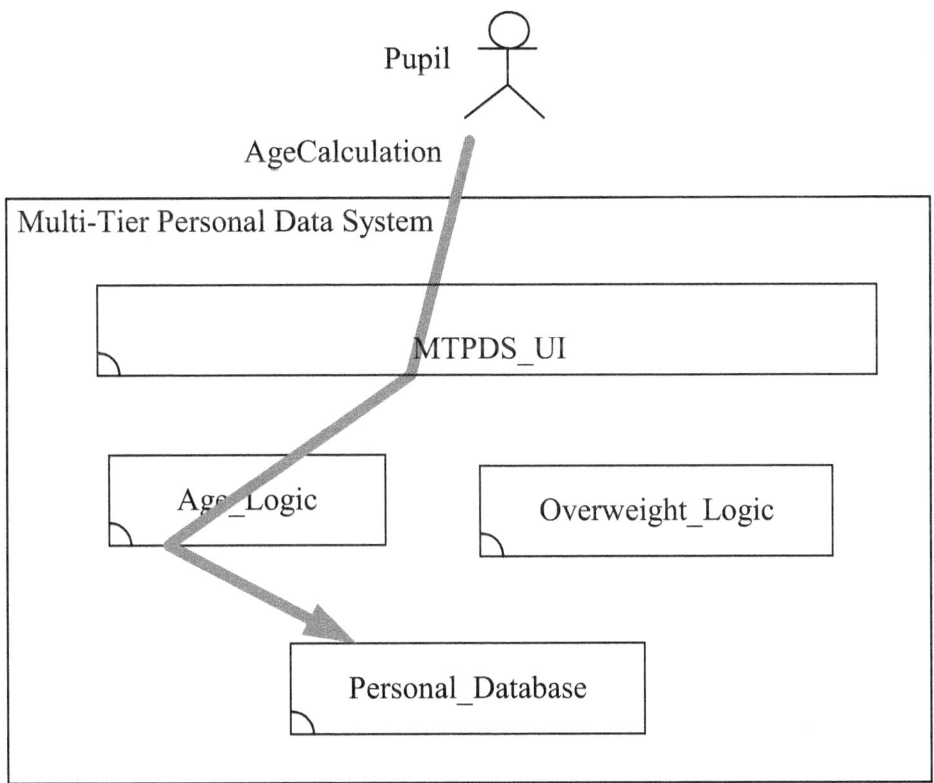

Figure 4-2. All Components, Actors, and the *AgeCalculation* Behavior

Adding the *OverweightCalculation* behavior to Figure 4-2, we then obtain the graphical representation shown in Figure 4-3. In this Figure, the *OverweightCalculation* behavior indicates that actor *Pupil* interacts with the *MTPDS_UI* component first, then component *MTPDS_UI* interacts with the *Overweight_Logic* component later, then component *Overweight_Logic* interacts with the *Personal_Database* component finally.

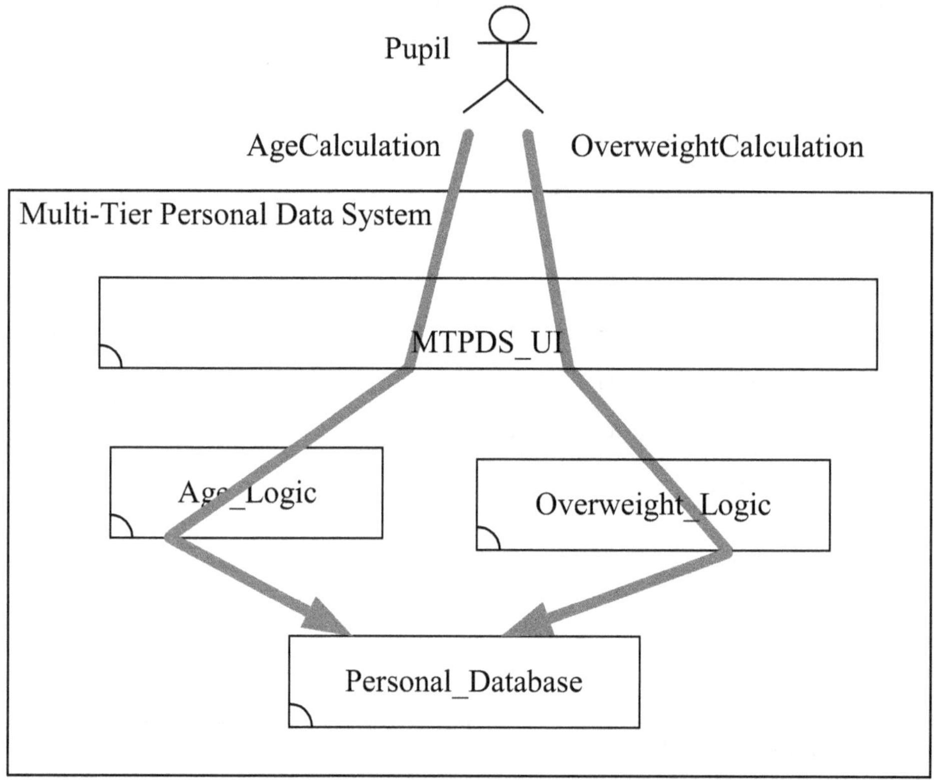

Figure 4-3. Adding the *OverweightCalculation* Behavior to Figure 4-2

After finishing Figure 4-3, we actually have accomplished all the works needed to draw an entire SBCD of the *Multi-Tier Personal Data System*. As a matter of fact, Figure 4-3 shows exactly the *Multi-Tier Personal Data System*'s SBCD.

4-2 Interaction Flow Diagram

An interaction flow diagram (IFD) is utilized to describe each individual behavior of the overall behavior of a system. IFD is the sixth fundamental diagram to achieve structure-behavior coalescence.

4-2-1 Individual Software Behavior Represented by Interaction Flow Diagram

The overall behavior of a system consists of many individual behaviors. Each individual behavior represents an execution path. An IFD is utilized to represent such an individual behavior.

Figure 4-4 demonstrates that the *Multi-Tier Personal Data System* has two behaviors; thus, it has two IFDs.

Enterprise	IFD
Multi-Tier Personal Data System	AgeCalculation
	OverweightCalculation

Figure 4-4. *Multi-Tier Personal Data System* has Two IFDs

4-2-2 Drawing the Interaction Flow Diagram

Let us now explain the usage of interaction flow diagram (IFD) by drawing an IFD step by step. Figure 4-5 demonstrates an IFD of the *SaleInput* behavior. The X-axis direction is from the left side to right side and the Y-axis direction is from the above to the below. Inside an IFD, there are four elements: a) external environment's actor, b) components, c) interactions and d) input/output parameters. Participants of the interaction, such as the external environment's actor and each component, are laid aside along the X-axis direction on the top of the diagram. The external environment's actor which initiates the sequential interactions is always placed on the most left side of the X-axis. Then, interactions among the external environment's actor and components successively in turn decorate along the Y-axis direction. The first interaction is placed on the top of the Y-axis position. The last interaction is placed on the bottom of the Y-axis position. Each interaction may carry several input and/or output parameters.

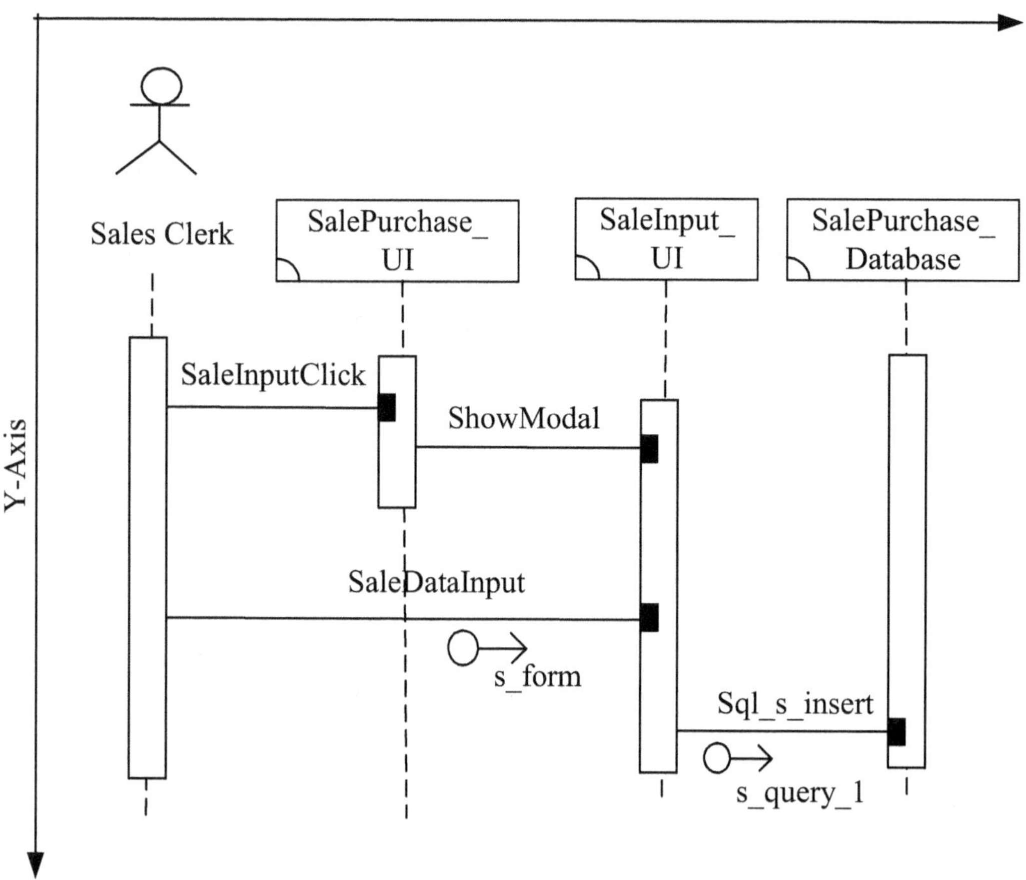

Figure 4-5. IFD of the *SaleInput* Behavior

In Figure 4-5, *Sales Clerk* is an external environment's actor. *SalePurchase_UI*, *SaleInput_UI* and *SalePurchase_Database* are components. *SaleInputClick* is an operation which is provided by the *SalePurchase_UI* component. *ShowModal* is an operation which is provided by the *SaleInput_UI* component. *SaleDataInput* is an operation, carrying the *s_form* input parameter, which is also provided by the *SaleInput_UI* component. *Sql_s_insert* is an operation, carrying the *s_query_1* input parameter, which is provided by the *SalePurchase_Database* component.

The execution path of Figure 4-5 is as follows. First, actor *Sales Clerk* interacts with the *SalePurchase_UI* component through the *SaleInputClick* operation call interaction. Next, component *SalePurchase_UI* interacts with the *SaleInput_UI* component through the *ShowModal* operation call interaction. Continuingly, actor *Sales Clerk* interacts with the *SaleInput_UI* component through the *SaleDataInput* operation call interaction, carrying the *s_form* input parameter. Finally, component *SaleInput_UI* interacts with the *SalePurchase_Database* component through the *Sql_s_insert* operation call interaction, carrying the *s_query_1* input parameter.

For each interaction, the solid line stands for operation call while the dashed line stands for operation return. The operation call and operation return interactions, if using the same operation name, belong to the identical operation. Figure 4-6 exhibits two interactions (operation call interaction and operation return interaction) having the identical "*Request*" operation.

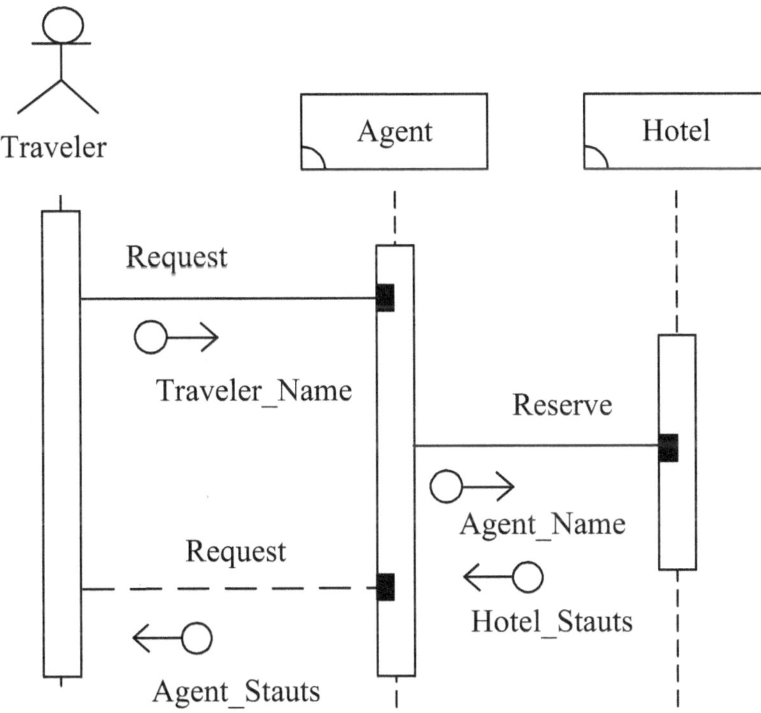

Figure 4-6. Two Interactions Have the Identical Operation

The execution path of Figure 4-6 is as follows. First, external environment's actor *Traveler* interacts with the *Agent* component through the *Request* operation call interaction, carrying the *Traveler_Name* input parameter. Next, component *Agent* interacts with the *Hotel* component through the *Reserve* operation call interaction, carrying the *Agent_Name* input parameter and *Hotel_Stauts* output parameter. Finally, external environment's actor *Traveler* interacts with the *Agent* component through the *Request* operation return interaction, carrying the

Agent_Stauts output parameter.

An interaction flow diagram may contain a conditional expression. Figure 4-7 shows such an example which has the following execution path. First, external environment's actor *Employee* interacts with the *Computer* component through the *Open* operation call interaction, carrying the *Task_No* input parameter. Next, if the *var_1 < 4 & var_2 > 7* condition is true then component *Computer* shall interact with the *Skype* component through the *Op_1* operation call interaction and component *Skype* shall interact with the *Earphone* component through the *Op_4* operation call interaction, carrying the *Skype_Earphone* output parameter; else if the *var_3 = 99* condition is true then component *Computer* shall interact with the *Skype* component through the *Op_2* operation call interaction and component *Skype* shall interact with the *Speaker* component through the *Op_5* operation call interaction, carrying the *Skype_Speaker* output parameter; else component *Computer* shall interact with the *Youtube* component through the *Op_3* operation call interaction and component *Youtube* shall interact with the *Speaker* component through the *Op_6* operation call interaction, carrying the *Youtube_Speaker* output parameter. Continuingly, if the *var_1 < 4 & var_2 > 7* condition is true then component *Computer* shall interact with the *Skype* component through the *Op_1* operation return interaction, carrying the *Status_1* output parameter; else if the *var_3 = 99* condition is true then component *Computer* shall interact with the *Skype* component through the *Op_2* operation return interaction, carrying the *Status_2* output parameter; else component *Computer* shall interact with the *Youtube* component through the *Op_3* operation return interaction, carrying the *Status_3* output parameter. Finally, external environment's actor *Employee* interacts with the *Computer* component through the *Open* operation return interaction, carrying the *Status* output parameter.

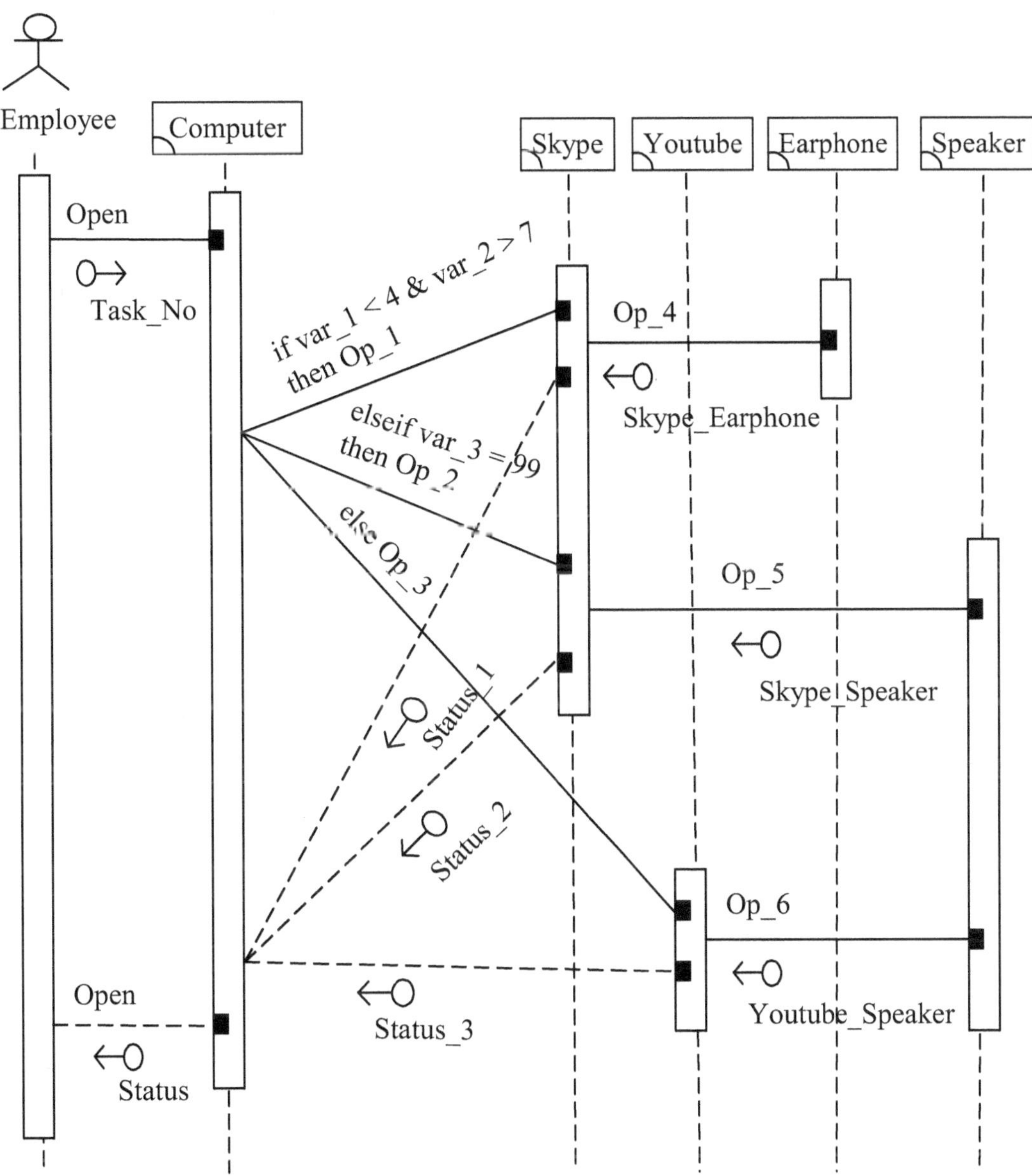

Figure 4-7. Conditional Interaction

Several Boolean conditions are shown in Figure 4-7. They are "*var_1 < 4 & var_2 > 7*" and "*var_3 = 99*". Variables, such as *var_1*, *var_2* and *var_3*, appearing in the Boolean condition can be local or global variables [Prat00, Seth96].

PART III: SOFTWARE ARCHITECTURE OF ONLINE SHOPPING SYSTEMS

Chapter 5: AHD of the Online Shopping System

AHD is the architecture hierarchy diagram we obtain after the architecture construction is finished. Figure 5-1 shows an AHD of the *Online Shopping System*. In the figure, *Online Shopping System* is composed of *User_Layer*, *Coordination_Layer* and *Service_Layer*; *User_Layer* is composed of *Customer_UI*, and *Supplier_UI*; *Coordination_Layer* is composed of *Customer_Coordinator*, *Supplier_Coordinator* and *Billing_Coordinator*; *Service_Layer* is composed of *Catalog_Service*, *Customer_Account_Service*, *Credit_Card_Service*, *Delivery_Order_Service*, *Email_Service* and *Inventory_Service*.

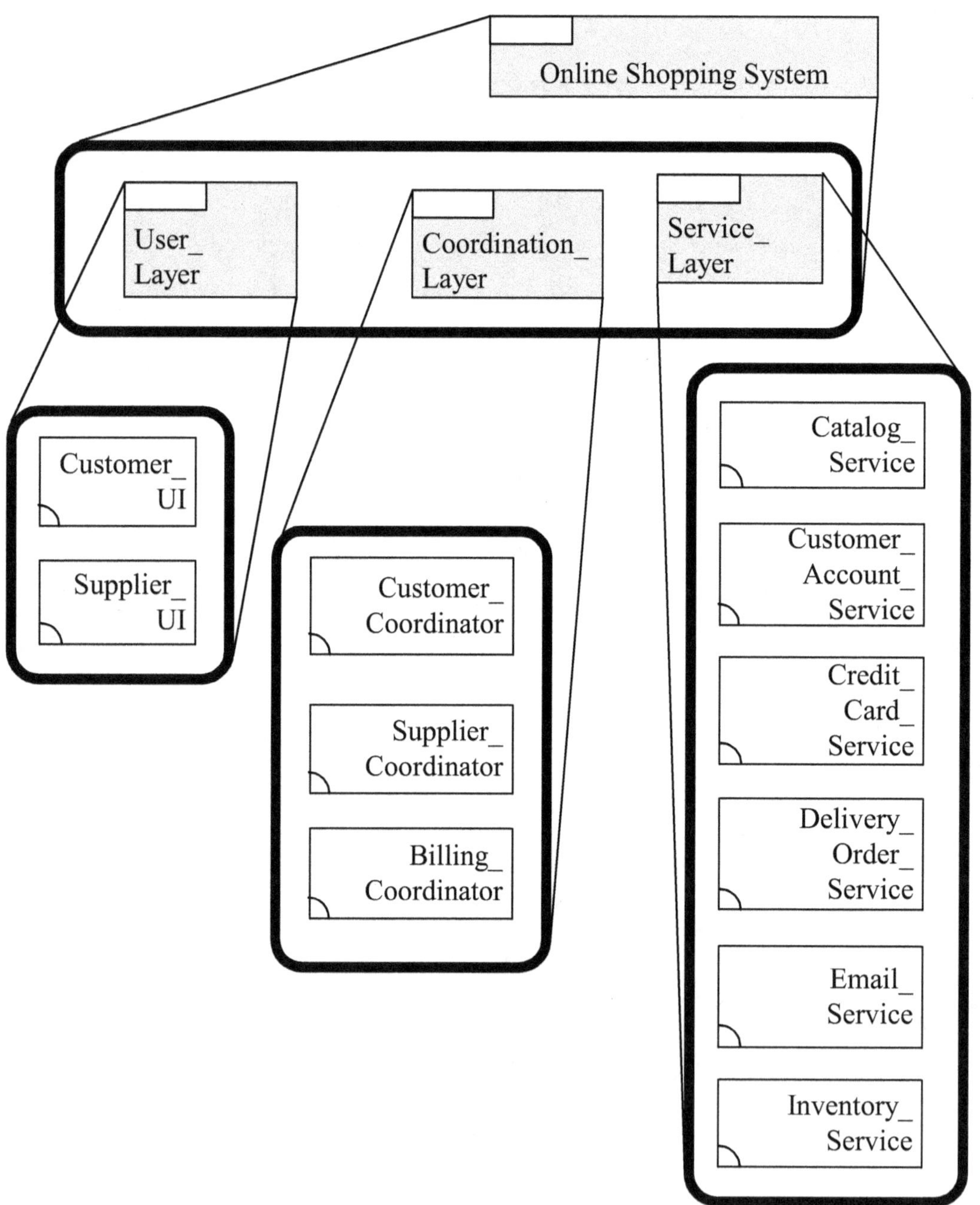

Figure 5-1. AHD of the *Online Shopping System*

In Figure 5-1, *Online Shopping System, User_Layer*, *Coordination_Layer* and *Service_Layer* are aggregated systems while *Customer_UI*, *Supplier_UI*, *Customer_Coordinator*, *Supplier_Coordinator*, *Billing_Coordinator*, *Catalog_Servicer*, *Customer_Account_Service*, *Credit_Card_Service*, *Delivery_Order_Service*, *Email_Service* and *Inventory_Service* are non-aggregated systems.

Chapter 6: FD of the Online Shopping System

FD is the framework diagram we obtain after the architecture construction is finished. Figure 6-1 shows the FD of the *Online Shopping System*.

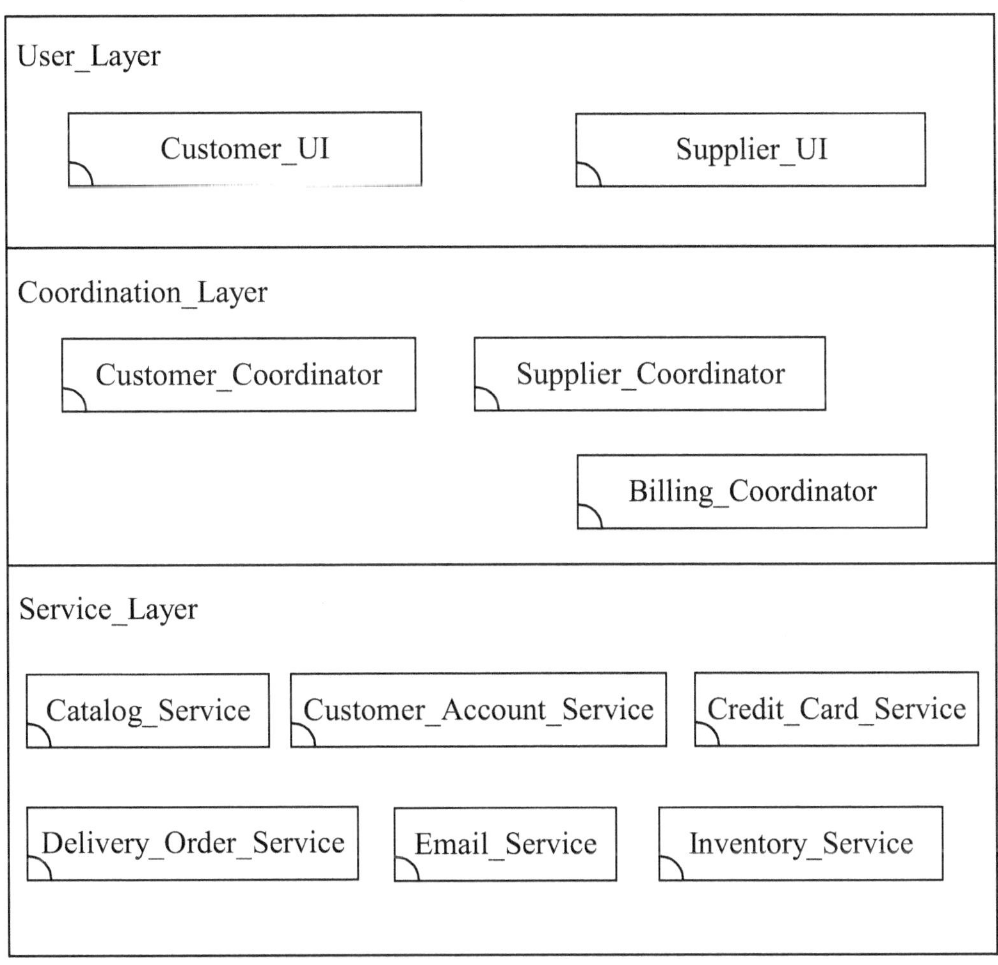

Figure 6-1. FD of the *Online Shopping System*

In the above figure, *User_Layer* contains the *Customer_UI* and *Supplier_UI* components; *Coordination_Layer* contains the *Customer_Coordinator*, *Supplier_Coordinator* and *Billing_Coordinator* components; *Service_Layer* contains the *Catalog_Servicer*, *Customer_Account_Service*, *Credit_Card_Service*, *Delivery_Order_Service*, *Email_Service* and *Inventory_Service* components.

Chapter 7: COD of the Online Shopping System

COD is the component operation diagram we obtain after the architecture construction is finished. Figure 7-1 shows a COD of the *Online Shopping System*. In the figure, component *Customer_UI* has four operations: *Request_Catalog_from_Customer*, *Request_Selection_from_Customer*, *Request_Order_from_Customer* and *Request_Order_Information_from_Customer*; component *Supplier_UI* has three operations: *Select_Order_from_Supplier*, *Reserve_Inventory_from_Supplier* and *Shipping*; component *Customer Coordinator* has four operations: *Request_Catalog_from_UI*, *Request Selection_from_UI*, *Request_Order_from_UI* and *Request_Order_Information_from_UI*; component *Supplier_Coordinator* has three operations: *Select_Order_from_UI*, *Reserve_Inventory_from_UI* and *Ready_for_Shippment*; component *Catalog_Service* has two operations: *Request_Catalog* and *Request_Selection*; component *Customer_Account_Service* has one operation: *Request_Account*; component *Credit_Card_Service* has two operations: *Authorize_Charge* and *Commit_Charge*; component *Delivery_Order_Service* has five operations: *Store_Order*, *Select_Order*, *Request_Invoice*, *Confirm_Payment* and *Read_Order*; component *Email_Service* has one operation: *Send_Email*; component *Inventory_Service* has three operations: *Check_Inventory*, *Reserve_Inventory* and *Commit_Inventory*.

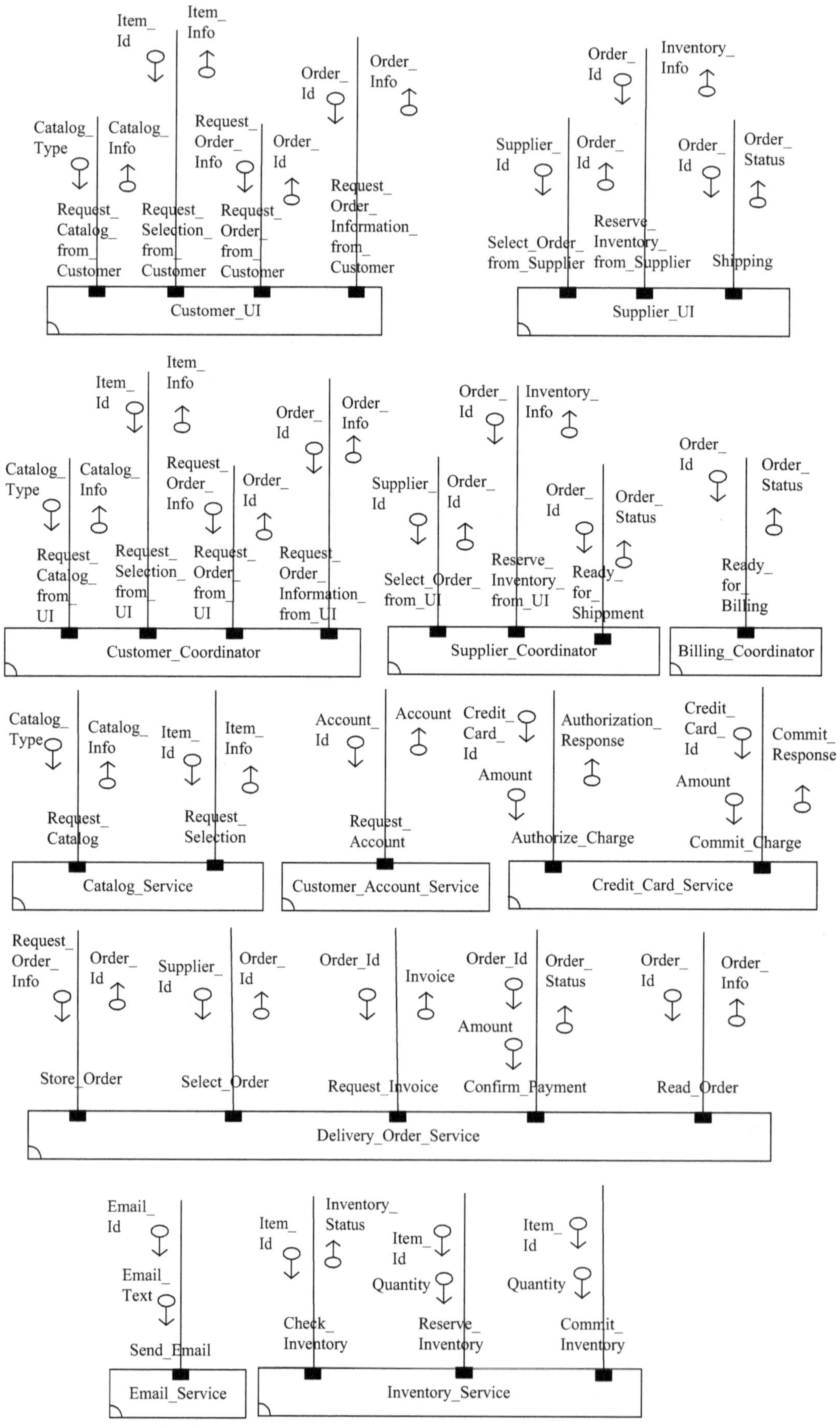

Figure 7-1. COD of the *Online Shopping System*

The operation formula of *Request_Catalog_from_Customer* is *Request_Catalog_from_Customer(In Catalog_Type; Out Catalog_Info*). The operation formula of *Request_Selection_from_Customer* is *Request_Selection_from_Customer(In Item_Id; Out Item_Info*). The operation formula of *Request_Order_from_Customer* is *Request_Order_from_Customer(In Request_Order_Info; Out Order_Id*). The operation formula of *Request_Order_Information_from_Customer* is *Request_Order_Information_from_Customer(In Order_Id; Out Order_Info*). The operation formula of *Select_Order_from_Supplier* is *Select_Order_from_Supplier(In Supplier_Id; Out Order_Id*). The operation formula of *Reserve_Inventory_from_Supplier* is *Reserve_Inventory_from_Supplier(In Order_Id; Out Inventory_Info*). The operation formula of *Shipping* is *Shipping(In Order_Id; Out Order_Status*). The operation formula of *Request_Catalog_from_UI* is *Request_Catalog_from_UI(In Catalog_Type; Out Catalog_Info*). The operation formula of *Request_Selection_from_UI* is *Request_Selection from UI(In Item_Id; Out Item_Info*). The operation formula of *Request_Order_from_UI* is *Request_Order_from_UI(In Request_Order_Info; Out Order_Id*). The operation formula of *Request_Order_Information_from_UI* is *Request_Order_Information_from_UI(In Order_Id; Out Order_Info*). The operation formula of *Select_Order_from_UI* is *Select_Order_from_UI(In Supplier_Id; Out Order_Id*). The operation formula of *Reserve_Inventory_from_UI* is *Reserve_Inventory_from_UI(In Order_Id; Out Inventory_Info*). The operation formula of *Ready_for_Shippment* is *Ready_for_Shippment(In Order_Id; Out Order_Status*). The operation formula of *Ready_for_Billing* is *Ready_for_Billing(In Order_Id; Out Order_Status*). The operation formula of *Request_Catalog* is *Request_Catalog(In Catalog_Type; Out Catalog_Info*). The operation formula of *Request_Selection* is *Request_Selection(In Item_Id; Out Item_Info*). The operation formula of *Request_Account* is *Request_Account(In Account_Id; Out Account*). The operation formula of *Authorize_Charge* is *Authorize_Charge(In Credit_Card_Id, Amount; Out Authorization_Response*). The operation formula of *Commit_Charge* is *Commit_Charge(In Credit_Card_Id, Amount; Out Commit_Response*). The operation formula of *Store_Order* is *Store_Order(In Request_Order_Info; Out Order_Id*). The operation formula of *Select_Order* is *Select_Order(In Supplier_Id; Out Order_Id*). The operation formula of *Request_Invoice* is *Request_Invoice(In Order_Id; Out Invoice*). The operation formula of *Confirm_Payment* is *Confirm_Payment(In Order_Id, Amount; Out Order_Status*). The operation formula of *Read_Order* is *Read_Order(In Order_Id; Out Order_Info*). The operation formula of *Send_Email* is *Send_Email(In Email_Id, Email_Text)*. The operation formula of *Check_Inventory* is *Check_Inventory(In Item_Id; Out Inventory_Status)*. The operation formula of *Reserve_Inventory* is *Reserve_Inventory(In Item_Id, Quantity)*. The operation formula of *Commit_Inventory* is *Commit_Inventory(In Item_Id, Quantity)*.

Figure 7-2 shows the primitive data type specification of the *Catalog_Type* input parameter occurring in the *Request_Catalog_from_Customer(In Catalog_Type; Out Catalog_Info)*, *Request_Catalog_from_UI(In Catalog_Type; Out Catalog_Info)* and *Request_Catalog(In Catalog_Type; Out Catalog_Info)* operation formulas.

Parameter	Data Type	Instances
Catalog_ Type	Catalog_Type_Enumeration = (Books, Computers, Home, Toys)	Books

Figure 7-2. Primitive Data Type Specification

Figure 7-3 shows the composite data type specification of the *Catalog_Info* output parameter occurring in the *Request_Catalog_from_Customer(In Catalog_Type; Out Catalog_Info)*, *Request_Catalog_from_UI(In Catalog_Type; Out Catalog_Info)* and *Request_Catalog(In Catalog_Type; Out Catalog_Info)* operation formulas.

<table>
<tr><td>Parameter</td><td>Catalog_Info</td></tr>
<tr><td>Data Type</td><td>TABLE of
Catalog_Id: Text
Catalog_Description: Text
Supplier_Id: Text
Catalog_Type: Catalog_Type_Enumeration
End TABLE ;</td></tr>
<tr><td>Instances</td><td><table>
<tr><th>Catalog_ Id</th><th>Catalog_ Description</th><th>Supplier_ Id</th><th>Catalog_Type</th></tr>
<tr><td>ABC001</td><td>Desktop PC</td><td>000003</td><td>Computers</td></tr>
<tr><td>ABC007</td><td>Toys for 3~6 years</td><td>000003</td><td>Toys</td></tr>
</table></td></tr>
</table>

Figure 7-3. Composite Data Type Specification of *Catalog_Info*

Figure 7-4 shows the primitive data type specification of the *Item_Id* input parameter occurring in the *Request_Selection_from_Customer(In Item_Id; Out Item_Info*), *Request_Selection_from_UI(In Item_Id; Out Item_Info*), *Request_Selection(In Item_Id; Out Item_Info*), *Check_Inventory(In Item_Id; Out Inventory_Status*), *Reserve_Inventory(In Item_Id, Quantity*) and *Commit_Inventory(In Item_Id, Quantity*) operation formulas.

Parameter	Data Type	Instances
Item_Id	Text	12345678

Figure 7-4. Primitive Data Type Specification

Figure 7-5 shows the composite data type specification of the *Item_Info* output parameter occurring in the *Request_Catalog_from_Customer(In Catalog_Type; Out Catalog_Info)*, *Request_Catalog_from_UI(In Catalog_Type; Out Catalog_Info)* and *Request_Catalog(In Catalog_Type; Out Catalog_Info)* operation formulas.

<table>
<tr><td>Parameter</td><td>Item_Info</td></tr>
<tr><td>Data Type</td><td>TABLE of
Item_Id: Text
Item_Description: Text
Unit_Cost: Real
Supplier_Id: Text
Item_Details: URL
End TABLE ;</td></tr>
<tr><td>Instances</td><td>
<table>
<tr><th>Item_ Id</th><th>Item_ Description</th><th>Unit_ Cost</th></tr>
<tr><td>12345678</td><td>Race Car</td><td>20.99</td></tr>
<tr><td>12341234</td><td>Airplane Toys</td><td>39.99</td></tr>
</table>
<table>
<tr><th>Supplier_ Id</th><th>Item_Details</th></tr>
<tr><td>000003</td><td>https://www.amazon.com/Cartoon-Toddlers-Liberty-Imports-Packaging/dp/B00G70DFC2</td></tr>
<tr><td>000008</td><td>https://www.rcmoment.com/p-rm8422.html?currency=TWD&Warehouse=CN</td></tr>
</table>
</td></tr>
</table>

Figure 7-5. Composite Data Type Specification of *Item_Info*

Figure 7-6 shows the composite data type specification of the *Request_Order_Info* input parameter occurring in the *Request_Order_from_Customer(In Request_Order_Info; Out Order_Id*), *Request_Order_from_UI(In Request_Order_Info; Out Order_Id*) and *Store_Order(In Request_Order_Info; Out Order_Id*) operation formula.

<table>
<tr><td>Parameter</td><td>Request_Order_Info</td></tr>
<tr><td>Data Type</td><td>TABLE of
Account_Id: Text
Item_Id: Text
Unit_Cost: Real
Quantity: Integer
End TABLE ;</td></tr>
<tr><td>Instances</td><td><table>
<tr><th>Account_ Id</th><th>Item_ Id</th><th>Unit_ Cost</th><th>Quantity</th></tr>
<tr><td>A234567</td><td>12345678</td><td>20.99</td><td>10</td></tr>
<tr><td>A234567</td><td>12341234</td><td>39.99</td><td>15</td></tr>
</table></td></tr>
</table>

Figure 7-6. Composite Data Type Specification of *Request_Order_Info*

Figure 7-7 shows the composite data type specification of the *Order_Info* output parameter occurring in the *Request_Order_Information_from_Customer(In Order_Id; Out Order_Info)*, *Request_Order_Information_from_UI(In Order_Id; Out Order_Info)* and *Read_Order(In Order_Id; Out Order_Info)* operation formulas.

<table>
<tr><td>Parameter</td><td>Order_Info</td></tr>
<tr><td>Data Type</td><td>TABLE of
Account_Id: Text
Item_Id: Text
Unit_Price Real
Quantity: Integer
Order_Status: Order_Status_Enumeration
Order_Id: Text
Supplier_Id: Text
End TABLE ;</td></tr>
<tr><td>Instances</td><td>
<table>
<tr><th>Account_ Id</th><th>Item_ Id</th><th>Unit_ Price</th><th>Quantity</th></tr>
<tr><td>22000001</td><td>12345678</td><td>20.99</td><td>10</td></tr>
<tr><td>22000001</td><td>12341234</td><td>39.99</td><td>15</td></tr>
</table>
<table>
<tr><th>Order_ Status</th><th>Order_ Id</th><th>Supplier_ Id</th></tr>
<tr><td>PreparedForShipment</td><td>201801030001</td><td>000003</td></tr>
<tr><td>PreparedForShipment</td><td>201801030001</td><td>000003</td></tr>
</table>
</td></tr>
</table>

Figure 7-7. Composite Data Type Specification of *Order_Info*

Figure 7-8 shows the primitive data type specification of the *Order_Id* parameter occurring in the *Request_Order_from_Customer(In Request_Order_Info; Out Order_Id*), *Request_Order_Information_from_Customer(In Order_Id; Out Order_Info*), *Select_Order_from_Supplier(In Supplier_Id; Out Order_Id*), *Reserve_Inventory_from_Supplier(In Order_Id; Out Inventory_Info*), *Shipping(In Order_Id; Out Order_Status*), *Request_Order_from_UI(In Request_Order_Info; Out Order_Id*), *Request_Order_Information_from_UI(In Order_Id; Out Order_Info*), *Select_Order_from_UI(In Supplier_Id; Out Order_Id*), *Reserve_Inventory_from_UI(In Order_Id; Out Inventory_Info*), *Ready_for_Shippment(In Order_Id; Out Order_Status*), *Ready_for_Billing(In Order_Id; Out Order_Status*), *Store_Order(In Request_Order_Info; Out Order_Id*), *Select_Order(In Supplier_Id; Out Order_Id*), *Request_Invoice(In Order_Id; Out Invoice*), *Confirm_Payment(In Order_Id, Amount; Out Order_Status*) and *Read_Order(In Order_Id; Out Order_Info*) operation formulas.

Parameter	Data Type	Instances
Order_Id	Text	201801030001

Figure 7-8. Primitive Data Type Specification

Figure 7-9 shows the primitive data type specification of the *Supplier_Id* input parameter occurring in the *Select_Order_from_Supplier(In Supplier_Id; Out Order_Id)*, *Select_Order_from_UI(In Supplier_Id; Out Order_Id)* and *Select_Order(In Supplier_Id; Out Order_Id)* operation formulas.

Parameter	Data Type	Instances
Supplier_Id	Text	000003

Figure 7-9. Primitive Data Type Specification

Figure 7-10 shows the composite data type specification of the *Inventory_Info* output parameter occurring in the *Reserve_Inventory_from_Supplier(In Order_Id; Out Inventory_Info*) and *Reserve_Inventory_from_UI(In Order_Id; Out Inventory_Info*) operation formulas.

<table>
<tr><td>Parameter</td><td>Inventory_Info</td></tr>
<tr><td>Data Type</td><td>TABLE of
Item_Id: Text
Item_Description: Text
Quantity: Integer
Quantity_Reserved: Integer
Unit_Price: Real
Reorder_Time: Date
End TABLE ;</td></tr>
<tr><td>Instances</td><td>
<table>
<tr><th>Item_ Id</th><th>Item_ Description</th><th>Quantity</th><th>Quantity_ Reserved</th></tr>
<tr><td>12345678</td><td>Race Car</td><td>1000</td><td>100</td></tr>
<tr><td>12341234</td><td>Airplane Toys</td><td>1500</td><td>100</td></tr>
</table>
<table>
<tr><th>Unit_ Price</th><th>Reorder_ Time</th></tr>
<tr><td>20.99</td><td>20180101</td></tr>
<tr><td>39.99</td><td>20180101</td></tr>
</table>
</td></tr>
</table>

Figure 7-10. Composite Data Type Specification of *Inventory_Info*

Figure 7-11 shows the primitive data type specification of the *Order_Status* output parameter occurring in the *Shipping(In Order_Id; Out Order_Status*), *Ready_for_Shippment(In Order_Id; Out Order_Status*), *Ready_for_Billing(In Order_Id; Out Order_Status*) and *Confirm_Payment(In Order_Id, Amount; Out Order_Status*) operation formulas.

Parameter	Data Type	Instances
Order_ Status	Order_Status_Enumeration = (NotYetShipped, PreparedForShipment, Shipped)	Shipped

Figure 7-11. Primitive Data Type Specification

Figure 7-12 shows the primitive data type specification of the *Account_Id* input parameter occurring in the *Request_Account(In Account_Id; Out Account*) operation formula.

Parameter	Data Type	Instances
Account_Id	Text	22000001

Figure 7-12. Primitive Data Type Specification

Figure 7-13 shows the composite data type specification of the *Account* output parameter occurring in the *Request_Account(In Account_Id; Out Account)* operation formula.

<table>
<tr><td>Parameter</td><td>Account</td></tr>
<tr><td>Data Type</td><td>TABLE of
Account_Id: Text
Email_Id: Text
Credit_Card_Id: Text
Credit_Card_Type: Text
Expiration_Date: Date
End TABLE ;</td></tr>
<tr><td>Instances</td><td>
<table>
<tr><td>Account_ Id</td><td>Email_ Id:</td></tr>
<tr><td>22000001</td><td>ammanusaimon@gmail.com</td></tr>
<tr><td>22000002</td><td>lilycollins@yahoo.com</td></tr>
</table>
<table>
<tr><td>Credit_ Card_ Id</td><td>Credit_ Card_ Type</td><td>Expiration_ Date</td></tr>
<tr><td>4000001234567899123</td><td>Prepaid</td><td>July 31, 2018</td></tr>
<tr><td>3137321345124890112</td><td>Standard</td><td>August 31, 2020</td></tr>
</table>
</td></tr>
</table>

Figure 7-13. Composite Data Type Specification of *Account*

Figure 7-14 shows the primitive data type specification of the *Credit_Card_Id* input parameter occurring in the *Authorize_Charge(In Credit_Card_Id, Amount; Out Authorization_Response)* and *Commit_Charge(In Credit_Card_Id, Amount; Out Commit_Response)* operation formulas.

Parameter	Data Type	Instances
Credit_ Card_ Id	Text	4000001234567899123

Figure 7-14. Primitive Data Type Specification

Figure 7-15 shows the primitive data type specification of the *Amount* input parameter occurring in the *Authorize_Charge(In Credit_Card_Id, Amount; Out Authorization_Response)*, *Commit_Charge(In Credit_Card_Id, Amount; Out Commit_Response)* and *Confirm_Payment(In Order_Id, Amount; Out Order_Status)*operation formulas.

Parameter	Data Type	Instances
Amount	Real	5223.99

Figure 7-15. Primitive Data Type Specification

Figure 7-16 shows the primitive data type specification of the *Authorization_Response* input parameter occurring in the *Authorize_Charge(In Credit_Card_Id, Amount; Out Authorization_Response)* operation formula.

Parameter	Data Type	Instances
Authorization_ Response	Text	5610591081018250

Figure 7-16. Primitive Data Type Specification

Figure 7-17 shows the primitive data type specification of the *Commit_Response* input parameter occurring in the *Commit_Charge(In Credit_Card_Id, Amount; Out Commit_Response)* operation formula.

Parameter	Data Type	Instances
Commit_ Response	Text	3566002020360505

Figure 7-17. Primitive Data Type Specification

Figure 7-18 shows the composite data type specification of the *Invoice* output parameter occurring in the *Request_Invoice(In Order_Id; Out Invoice)*operation formula.

<table>
<tr><td>Parameter</td><td>Invoice</td></tr>
<tr><td>Data Type</td><td>TABLE of
Order_Id: Text
Account_Id: Text
Amount_Due: Real
Actual_Ship_Date: Date
Authorization_Id: Text
End TABLE ;</td></tr>
<tr><td>Instances</td><td>
<table>
<tr><td>Order_ Id</td><td>Account_ Id</td><td>Amount_ Due</td></tr>
<tr><td>201801030001</td><td>22000001</td><td>400.99</td></tr>
<tr><td>201801030001</td><td>22000001</td><td>200.99</td></tr>
</table>
<table>
<tr><td>Actual_ Ship_ Date</td><td>Authorization_ Id</td></tr>
<tr><td>20180101</td><td>000000001</td></tr>
<tr><td>20180103</td><td>000000001</td></tr>
</table>
</td></tr>
</table>

Figure 7-18. Composite Data Type Specification of *Invoice*

Figure 7-19 shows the primitive data type specification of the *Email_Id* input parameter occurring in the *Send_Email(In Email_Id, Email_Text)* operation formula.

Parameter	Data Type	Instances
Email_Id	Text	ammanusaimon@gmail.com

Figure 7-19. Primitive Data Type Specification

Figure 7-20 shows the primitive data type specification of the *Email_Text* input parameter occurring in the *Send_Email(In Email_Id, Email_Text)* operation formula.

Parameter	Data Type	Instances
Email_Text	Text	Your order has been acknowledged. We will deliver your order as soon as possible. Keep in touch.

Figure 7-20. Primitive Data Type Specification

Figure 7-21 shows the composite data type specification of the *Inventory_Status* output parameter occurring in the *Check_Inventory(In Item_Id; Out Inventory_Status*) operation formula.

<table>
<tr><td>Parameter</td><td>Inventory_Status</td></tr>
<tr><td>Data Type</td><td>TABLE of
Item_Id: Text
Current_Quantity: Integer
Quantity_After_Shipped: Integer
Reorder_time: Date
End TABLE ;</td></tr>
<tr><td>Instances</td><td><table>
<tr><td>Item_ Id</td><td>Current_ Quantity</td><td>Quantity_ After_ Shipped:</td><td>Reorder_ Time</td></tr>
<tr><td>12345678</td><td>2000</td><td>1000</td><td>20180101</td></tr>
<tr><td>12341234</td><td>2000</td><td>1500</td><td>20180101</td></tr>
</table></td></tr>
</table>

Figure 7-21. Composite Data Type Specification of *Inventory_Status*

Figure 7-22 shows the primitive data type specification of the *Quantity* input parameter occurring in the *Reserve_Inventory(In Item_Id, Quantity*) and *Commit_Inventory(In Item_Id, Quantity*) operation formulas.

Parameter	Data Type	Instances
Quantity	Integer	500

Figure 7-22. Primitive Data Type Specification

Chapter 8: CCD of the Online Shopping System

CCD is the component connection diagram we obtain after the architecture construction is finished. Figure 8-1 shows a CCD of the *Online Shopping System*.

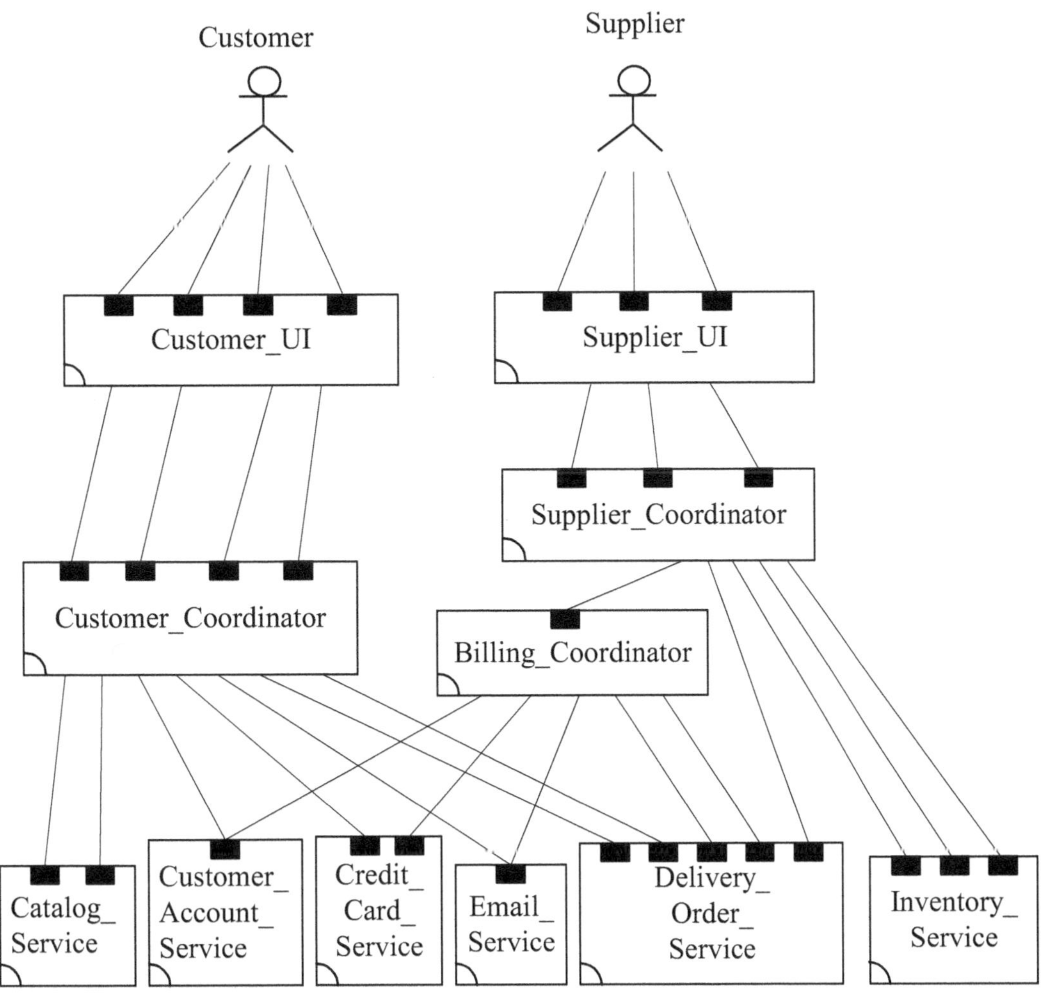

Figure 8-1. CCD of the *Online Shopping System*

In the above figure, actor *Customer* has four connections with the *Customer_UI* component; actor *Supplier* has three connections with the *Supplier_UI* component; component *Customer_UI* has four connections with the *Customer_Coordinator* component; component *Supplier_UI* has three connections with the *Supplier_Coordinator* component; component *Customer_Coordinator* has two connections with the *Catalog_Service* component; component *Customer_Coordinator* has a connection with each one of the *Customer_Account_Service*, *Credit_Card_Service*, *Email_Service* components; component *Customer_Coordinator* has two connections with the *Delivery_Order_Service* component; component *Supplier_Coordinator* has a connection with the *Billing_Coordinator* component; component *Supplier_Coordinator* has a connection with the *Delivery_Order_Service* component; component *Supplier_Coordinator* has three connections with the *Inventory_Service* component; component *Billing_Coordinator* has a connection with each one of the *Customer_Account_Service*, *Credit_Card_Service*, *Email_Service* components; component *Billing_Coordinator* has two connections with the *Delivery_Order_Service* component.

Chapter 9: SBCD of the Online Shopping System

SBCD is the structure-behavior coalescence diagram we obtain after the architecture construction is finished. Figure 9-1 shows a SBCD of the *Online Shopping System* in which interactions among the *Customer*, *Supplier* actors and the *Customer_UI*, *Supplier_UI*, *Customer_Coordinator*, *Supplier_Coordinator*, *Billing_Coordinator*, *Catalog_Servicer*, *Customer_Account_Service*, *Credit_Card_Service*, *Delivery_Order_Service*, *Email_Service*, *Inventory_Service* components shall draw forth the *Browse_Catalog*, *Make_Order_Request*, *Process_Delivery_Order*, *Confirm_Shipment_and_Bill_Customer*, *View_Order* behaviors.

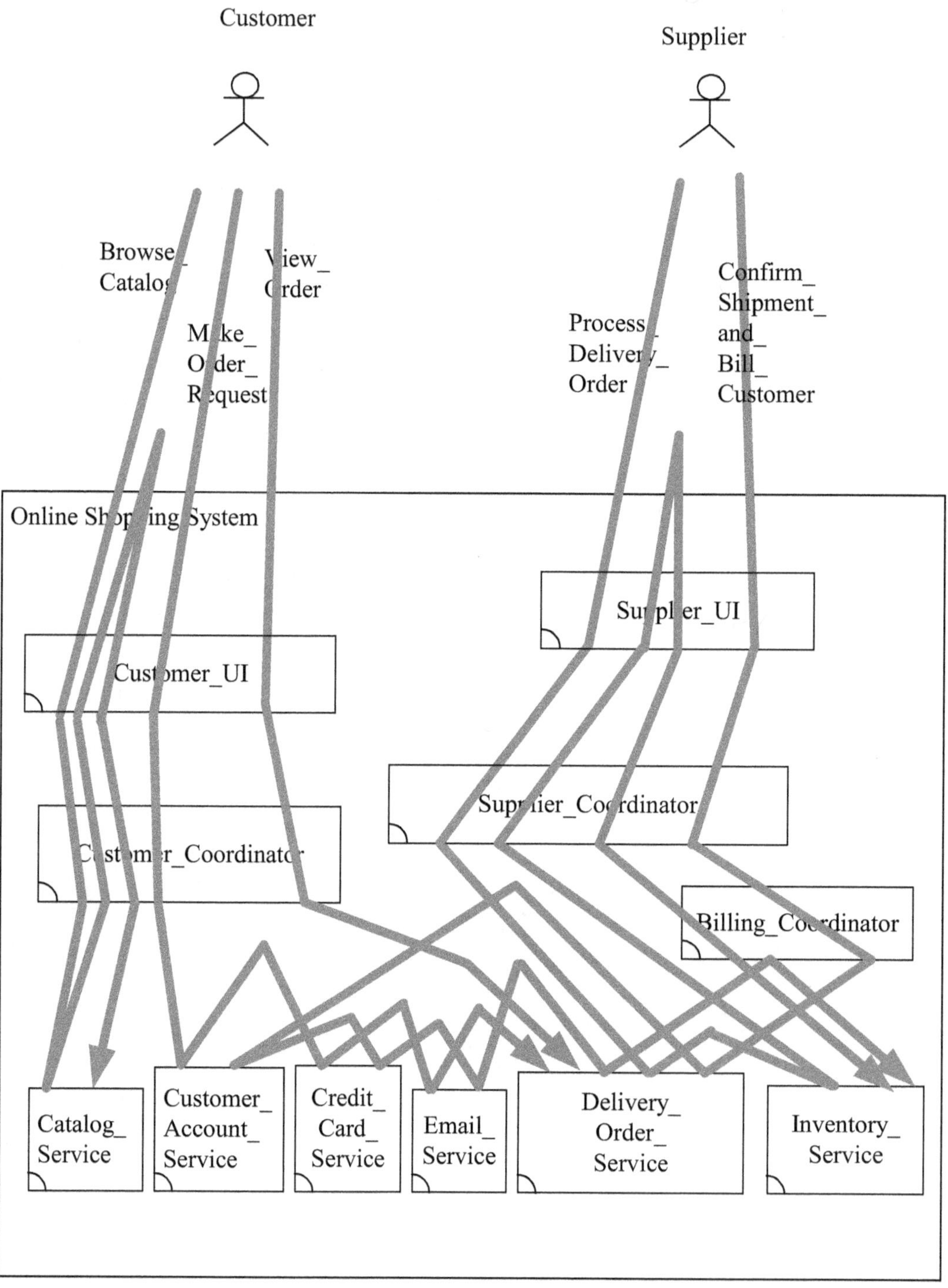

Figure 9-1. SBCD of the *Online Shopping System*

The overall behavior of the *Online Shopping System* includes the *Browse_Catalog*, *Make_Order_Request*, *Process_Delivery_Order*, *Confirm_Shipment_and_Bill_Customer*, *View_Order* behaviors. In other words, the *Browse_Catalog*, *Make_Order_Request*, *Process_Delivery_Order*, *Confirm_Shipment_and_Bill_Customer*, *View_Order* behaviors together provide the overall behavior of the *Online Shopping System*.

The major purpose of adopting the architectural approach, instead of separating the structure model from the behavior model, is to achieve one single coalesced model. In Figure 9-1, software architects are able to see that the software structure and software behavior coexist in the SBCD. That is, in the SBCD of the *Online Shopping System*, software architects not only see its software structure but also see (at the same time) its software behavior.

Chapter 10: IFD of the Online Shopping System

IFDs are the interaction flow diagrams we obtain after the architecture construction is finished. The overall behavior of the *Online Shopping System* includes five individual behaviors: *Browse_Catalog*, *Make_Order_Request*, *Process_Delivery_Order*, *Confirm_Shipment_and_Bill_Customer*, *View_Order*.

Figure 10-1 shows an IFD of the *Browse_Catalog*, behavior. First, actor *Customer* interacts with the *Customer_UI* component through the *Request_Catalog_from_Customer* operation call interaction, carrying the *Catalog_Type* input parameter. Next, component *Customer_UI* interacts with the *Customer_Coordinator* component through the *Request_Catalog_from_UI* operation call interaction, carrying the *Catalog_Type* input parameter. Continuingly, component *Customer_Coordinator* interacts with the *Catalog_Service* component through the *Request_Catalog* operation call interaction, carrying the *Catalog_Type* input parameter and *Catalog_Info* output parameter. Continuingly, component *Customer_UI* interacts with the *Customer_Coordinator* component through the *Request_Catalog_from_UI* operation return interaction, carrying the *Catalog_Info* output parameter. Continuingly, actor *Customer* interacts with the *Customer_UI* component through the *Request_Catalog_from_Customer* operation return interaction, carrying the *Catalog_Info* output parameter. Continuingly, actor *Customer* interacts with the *Customer_UI* component through the *Request_Selection_from_Customer* operation call interaction, carrying the *Item_Id* input parameter. Next, component *Customer_UI* interacts with the *Customer_Coordinator* component through the *Request_Selection_from_UI* operation call interaction, carrying the *Item_Id* input parameter. Continuingly, component *Customer_Coordinator* interacts with the *Catalog_Service* component through the *Request_Selection* operation call interaction, carrying the *Item_Id* input parameter and *Item_Info* output parameter. Continuingly, component *Customer_UI* interacts with the *Customer_Coordinator* component through the *Request_Selection_from_UI* operation return interaction, carrying the *Item_Info* output parameter. Finally, actor *Customer* interacts with the *Customer_UI* component through the *Request_Selection_from_Customer* operation return interaction, carrying the *Item_Info* output parameter.

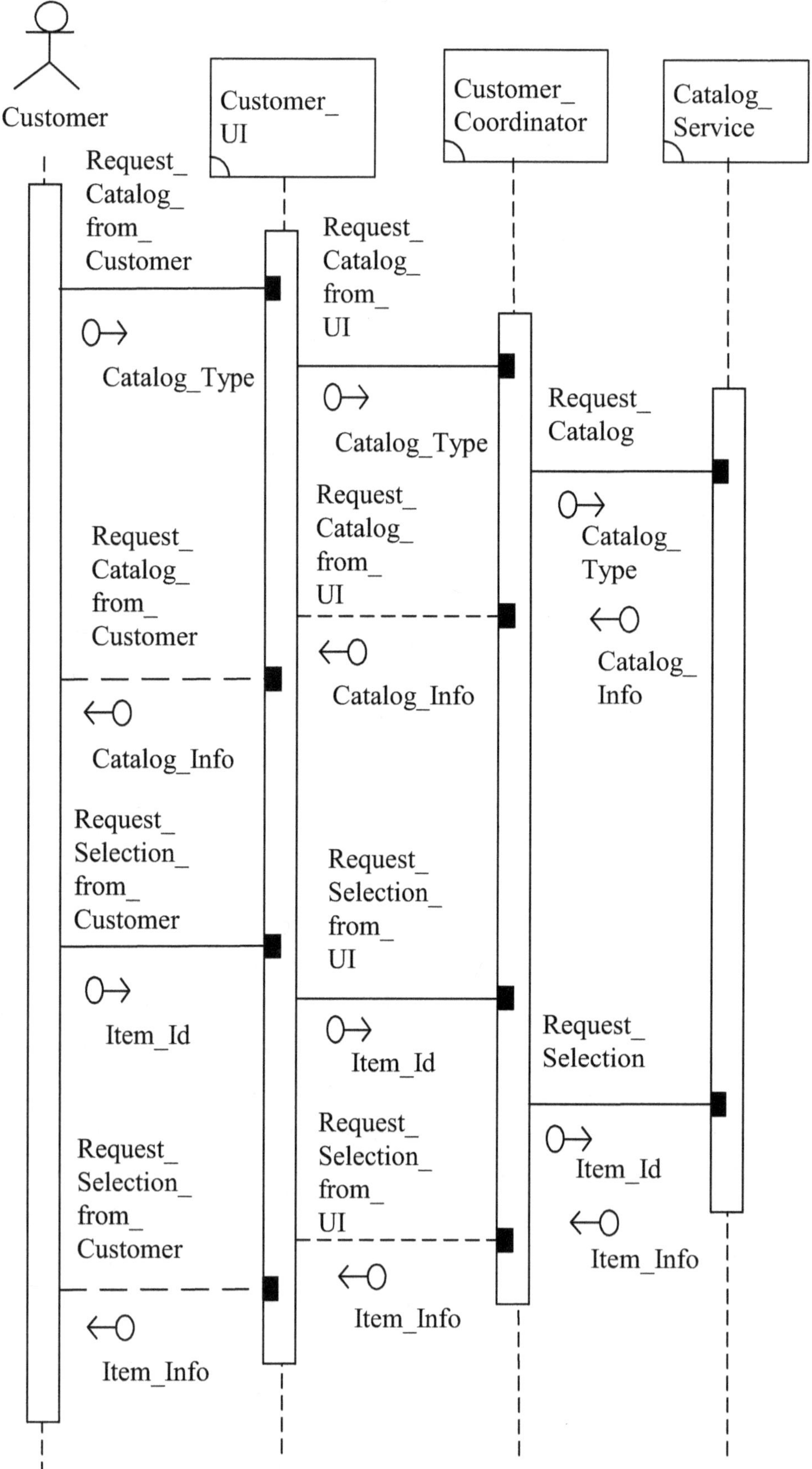

Figure 10-1. IFD of the *Browse_Catalog* Behavior

Figure 10-2 shows an IFD of the *Make_Order_Request* behavior. First, actor *Customer* interacts with the *Customer_UI* component through the *Request_Order_from_Customer* operation call interaction, carrying the *Request_Order_Info* input parameter. Next, component *Customer_UI* interacts with the *Customer_Coordinator* component through the *Request_Order_from_UI* operation call interaction, carrying the *Request_Order_Info* input parameter. Continuingly, component *Customer_Coordinator* interacts with the *Customer_Account_Service* component through the *Request_Account* operation call interaction, carrying the *Account_Id* input parameter and *Account* output parameter. Continuingly, component *Customer_Coordinator* interacts with the *Credit_Card_Service* component through the *Authorize_Charge* operation call interaction, carrying the *Credit_Card_Id*, *Amount* input parameters and *Authorization_Response* output parameter. Continuingly, component *Customer_Coordinator* interacts with the *Delivery_Order_Service* component through the *Store_Order* operation call interaction, carrying the *Request_Order_Info* input parameter and *Order_Id* output parameter. Continuingly, component *Customer_Coordinator* interacts with the *Email_Service* component through the *Send_Email* operation call interaction, carrying the *Email_Id*, *Email_Text* input parameters. Continuingly, component *Customer_UI* interacts with the *Customer_Coordinator* component through the *Request_Order_from_UI* operation return interaction, carrying the *Order_Id* output parameter. Last, actor *Customer* interacts with the *Customer_UI* component through the *Request_Order_from_Customer* operation return interaction, carrying the *Order_Id* output parameter.

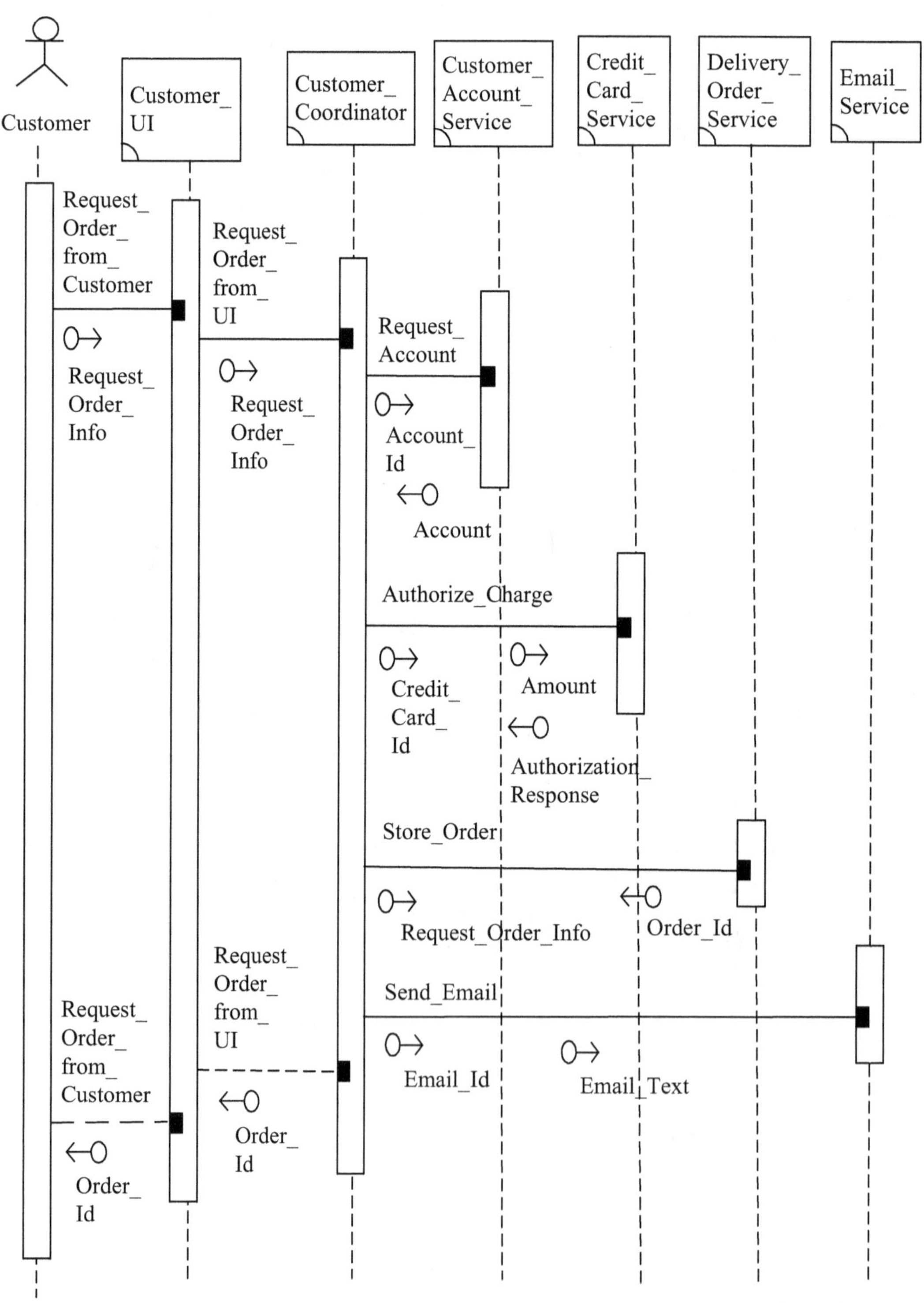

Figure 10-2. IFD of the *Make_Order_Request* Behavior

Figure 10-3 shows an IFD of the *Process_Delivery_Order* behavior. First, actor *Supplier* interacts with the *Supplier_UI* component through the *Select_Order_from_Supplier* operation call interaction, carrying the *Supplier_Id* input parameter. Next, component *Supplier_UI* interacts with the *Supplier_Coordinator* component through the *Select_Order_from_UI* operation call interaction, carrying the *Supplier_Id* input parameter. Continuingly, component *Supplier_Coordinator* interacts with the *Delivery_Order_Service* component through the *Select_Order* operation call interaction, carrying the *Supplier_Id* input parameter and *Order_Id* output parameter. Continuingly, component *Supplier_Coordinator* interacts with the *Inventory_Service* component through the *Check_Inventory* operation call interaction, carrying the *Item_Id* input parameter and *Inventory_Status* output parameter. Continuingly, component *Supplier_UI* interacts with the *Supplier_Coordinator* component through the *Select_Order_from_UI* operation return interaction, carrying the *Order_Id* output parameter. Continuingly, actor *Supplier* interacts with the *Supplier_UI* component through the *Select_Order_from_Supplier* operation return interaction, carrying the *Order_Id* output parameter. Next, actor *Supplier* interacts with the *Supplier_UI* component through the *Reserve_Inventory_from_Supplier* operation call interaction, carrying the *Order_Id* input parameter. Continuingly, component *Supplier_UI* interacts with the *Supplier_Coordinator* component through the *Reserve_Inventory_from_UI* operation call interaction, carrying the *Order_Id* input parameter. Continuingly, component *Supplier_Coordinator* interacts with the *Inventory_Service* component through the *Check_Inventory* operation call interaction, carrying the *Item_Id*, *Quantity* input parameters. Continuingly, component *Supplier_UI* interacts with the *Supplier_Coordinator* component through the *Select_Order_from_UI* operation return interaction, carrying the *Inventory_Info* output parameter. Finally, actor *Supplier* interacts with the *Supplier_UI* component through the *Reserve_Inventory_from_Supplier* operation return interaction, carrying the *Inventory_Info* output parameter.

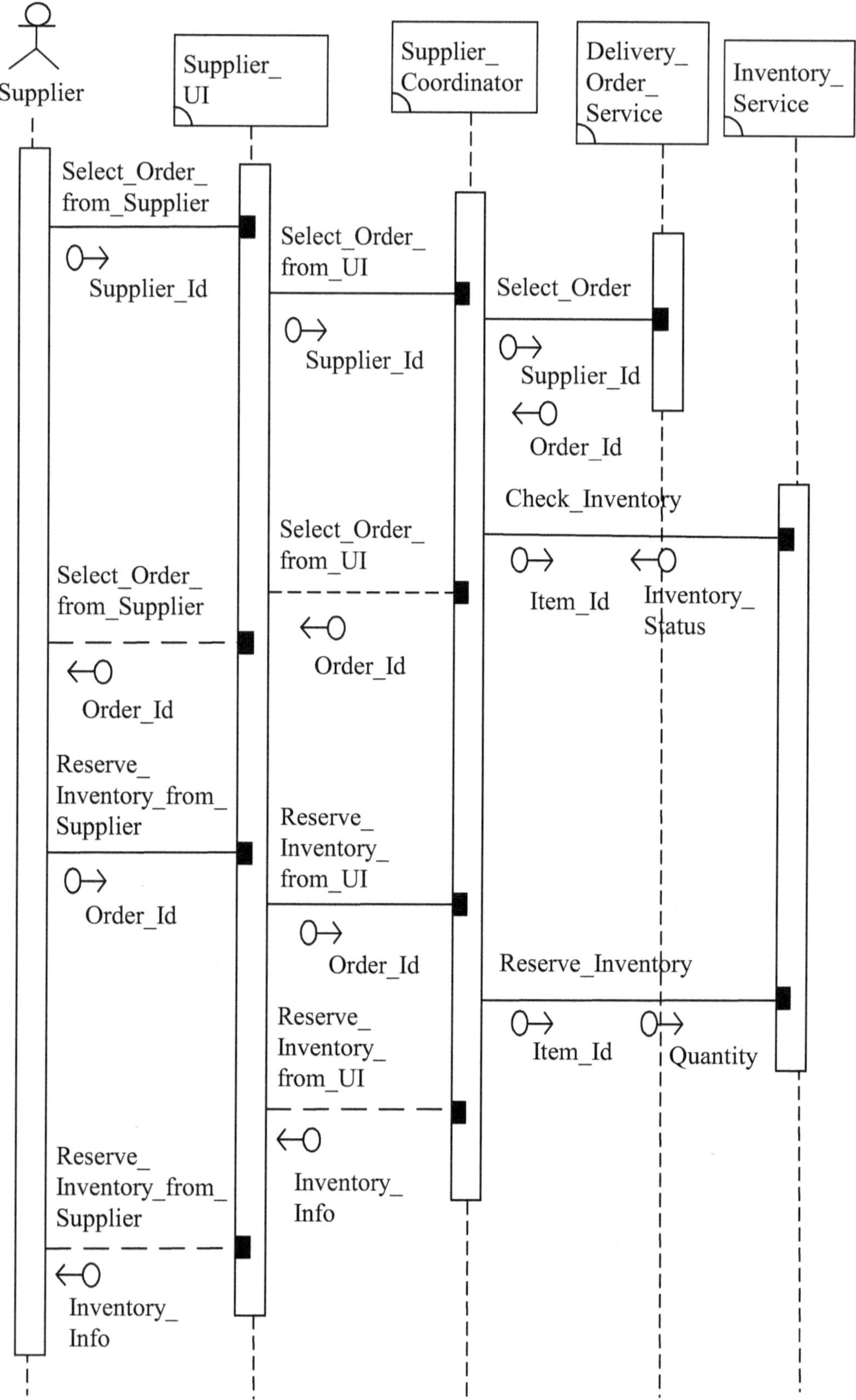

Figure 10-3. IFD of the *Process_Delivery_Order* Behavior

Figure 10-4 shows an IFD of the *Confirm_Shipment_and_Bill_Customer* behavior. First, actor *Supplier* interacts with the *Supplier_UI* component through the *Shipping* operation call interaction, carrying the *Order_Id* input parameter. Next, component *Supplier_UI* interacts with the *Supplier_Coordinator* component through the *Ready_for_Shippment* operation call interaction, carrying the *Order_Id* input parameter. Continuingly, component *Supplier_Coordinator* interacts with the *Billing_Coordinator* component through the *Ready_for_Billing* operation call interaction, carrying the *Order_Id* input parameter. Continuingly, component *Billing_Coordinator* interacts with the *Delivery_Order_Service* component through the *Request_Invoice* operation call interaction, carrying the *Order_Id* input parameter and *Invoice* output parameter. Continuingly, component *Billing_Coordinator* interacts with the *Customer_Account_Service* component through the *Request_Account* operation call interaction, carrying the *Account_Id* input parameter and *Account* output parameter. Continuingly, component *Billing_Coordinator* interacts with the *Credit_Card_Service* component through the *Commit_Charge* operation call interaction, carrying the *Credit_Card_Id*, *Amount* input parameters and *Commit_Response* output parameter. Continuingly, component *Billing_Coordinator* interacts with the *Delivery_Order_Service* component through the *Confirm_Payment* operation call interaction, carrying the *Order_Id*, *Amount* input parameters and *Order_Status* output parameter. Next, component *Billing_Coordinator* interacts with the *Email_Service* component through the *Send_Email* operation call interaction, carrying the *Email_Id*, *Email_Text* input parameters. Continuingly, component *Supplier_Coordinator* interacts with the *Billing_Coordinator* component through the *Ready_for_Billing* operation return interaction, carrying the *Order_Status* output parameter. Continuingly, component *Supplier_Coordinator* interacts with the *Inventory_Service* component through the *Commit_Inventory* operation call interaction, carrying the *Item_Id*, *Quantity* input parameters. Continuingly, component *Supplier_UI* interacts with the *Supplier_Coordinator* component through the *Ready_for_Shippment* operation return interaction, carrying the *Order_Status* output parameter. Last, actor *Supplier* interacts with the *Supplier_UI* component through the *Shipping* operation return interaction, carrying the *Order_Status* output parameter.

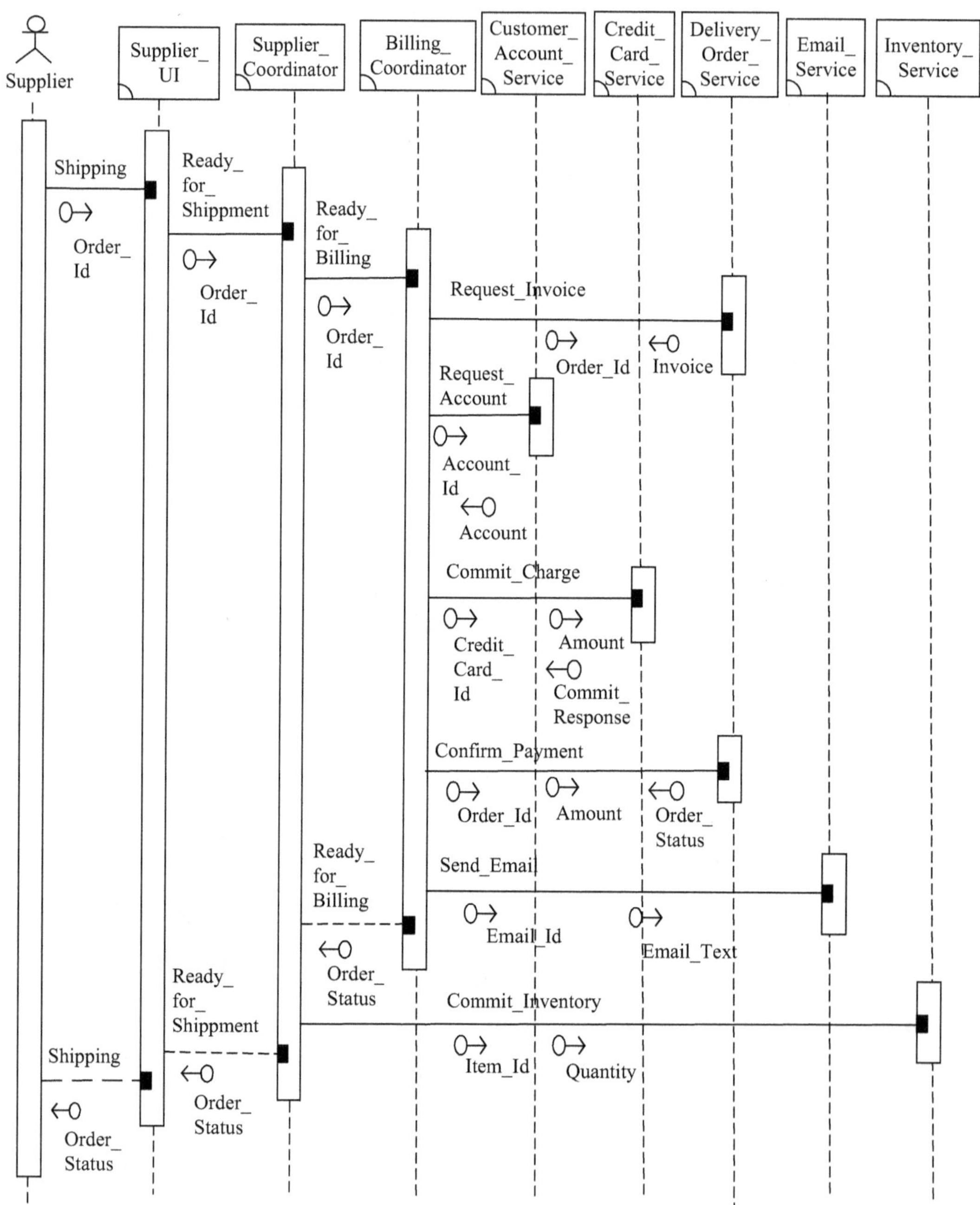

Figure 10-4. IFD of the *Confirm_Shipment_and_Bill_Customer* Behavior

Figure 10-5 shows an IFD of the *View_Order* behavior. First, actor *Customer* interacts with the *Customer_UI* component through the *Request_Order_Information_from_Customer* operation call interaction, carrying the *Order_Id* input parameter. Next, component *Customer_UI* interacts with the *Customer_Coordinator* component through the *Request_Order_Information_from_UI* operation call interaction, carrying the *Order_Id* input parameter. Continuingly, component *Customer_Coordinator* interacts with the *Delivery_Order_Service* component through the *Read_Order* operation call interaction, carrying the *Order_Id* input parameter and *Order_Info* output parameter. Continuingly, component *Customer_UI* interacts with the *Customer_Coordinator* component through the *Request_Order_Information_from_UI* operation return interaction, carrying the *Order_Info* output parameter. Last, actor *Customer* interacts with the *Customer_UI* component through the *Request_Order_Information_from_Customer* operation return interaction, carrying the *Order_Info* output parameter.

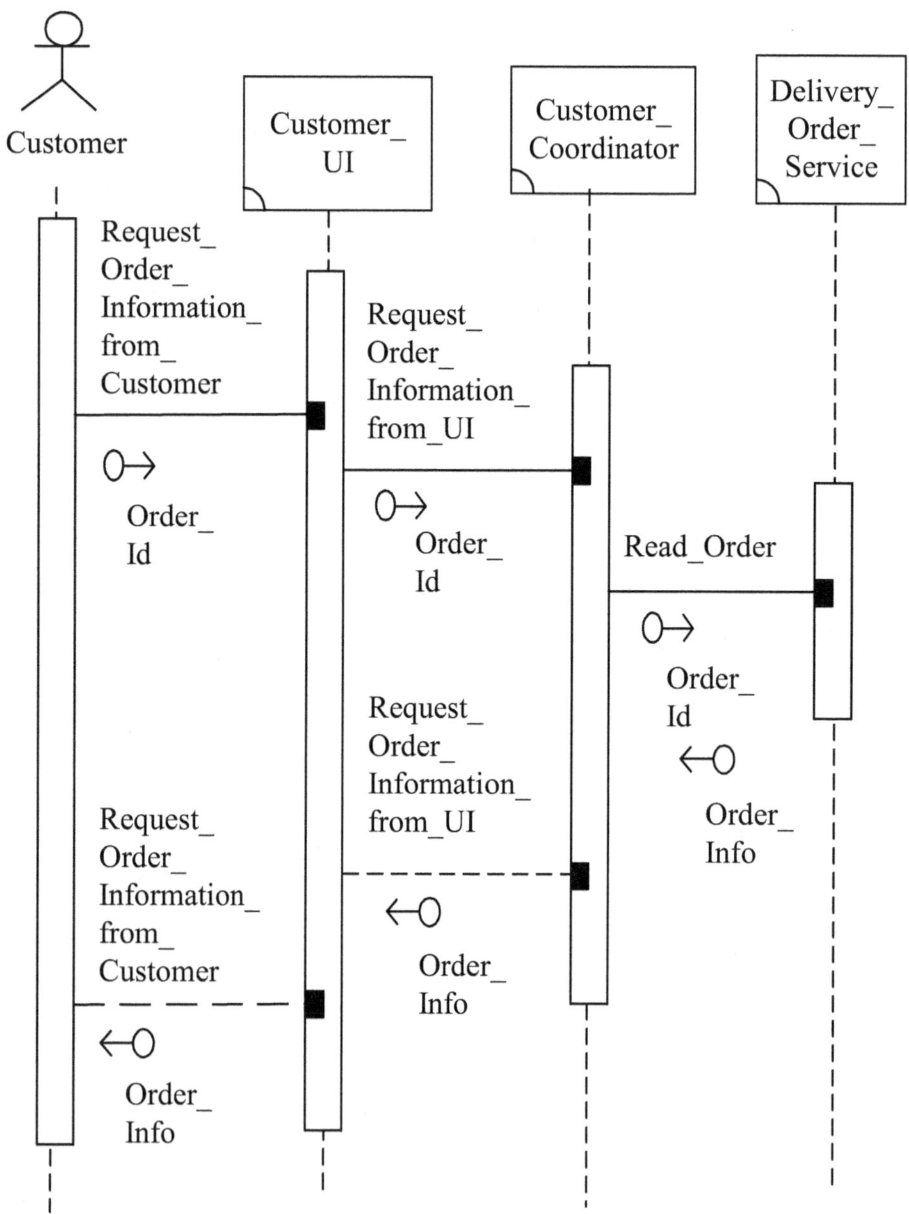

Figure 10-5. IFD of the *View_Order* Behavior

APPENDIX A: SBC ARCHITECTURE DESCRIPTION LANGUAGE

(1) Architecture Hierarchy Diagram

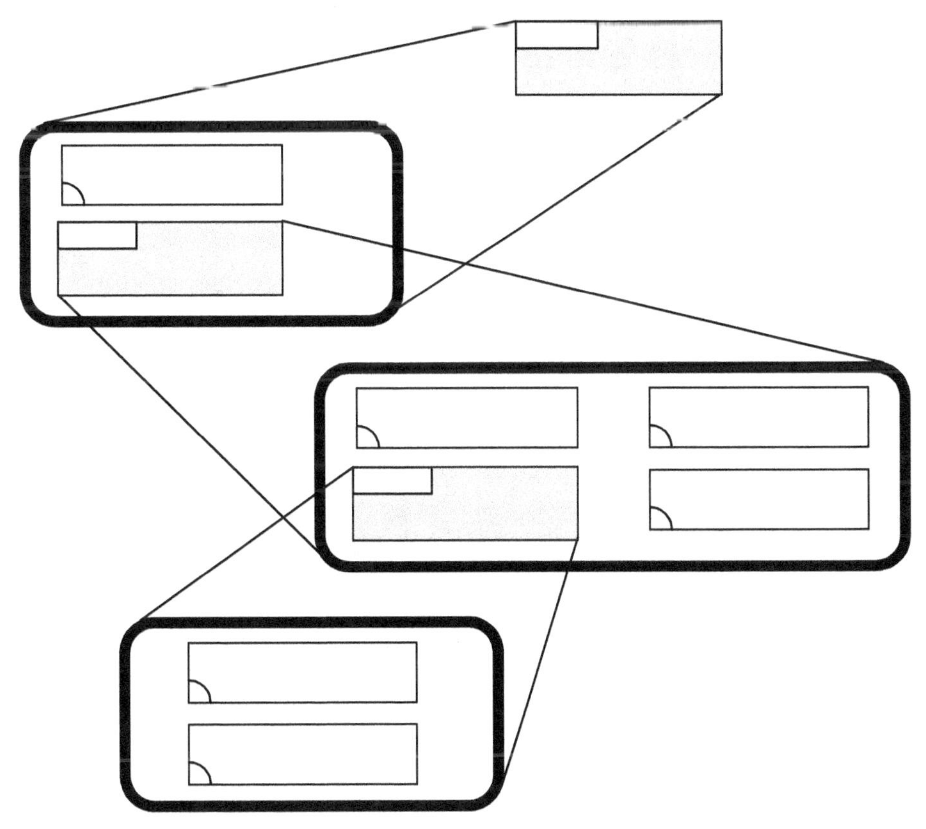

: Aggregated System

: Non-Aggregated System, Component

(2) Framework Diagram

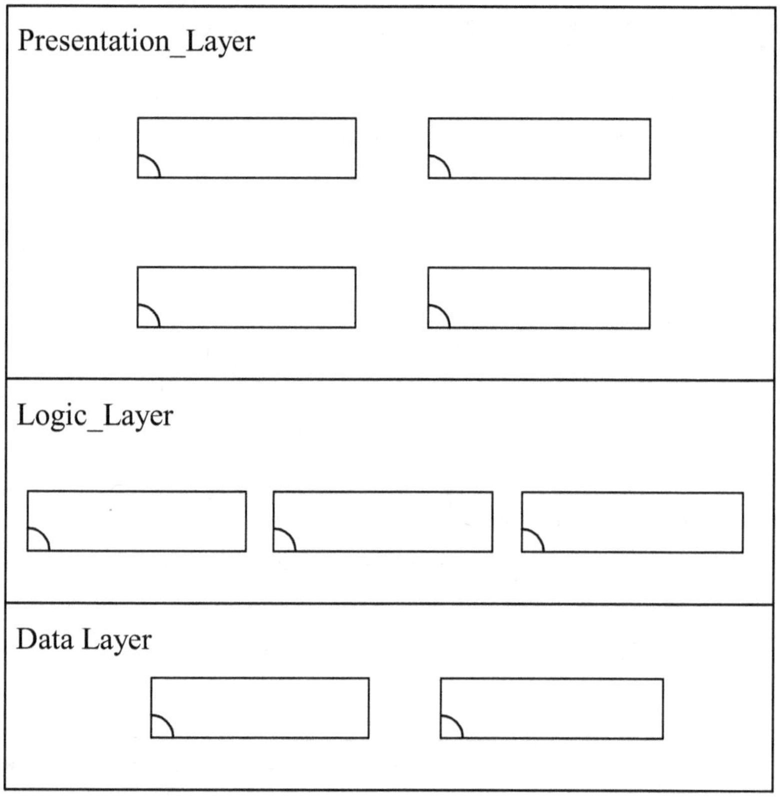

Presentation_Layer

Logic_Layer

Data Layer

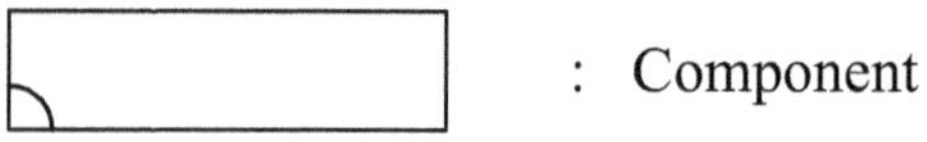

: Component

(3) Component Operation Diagram

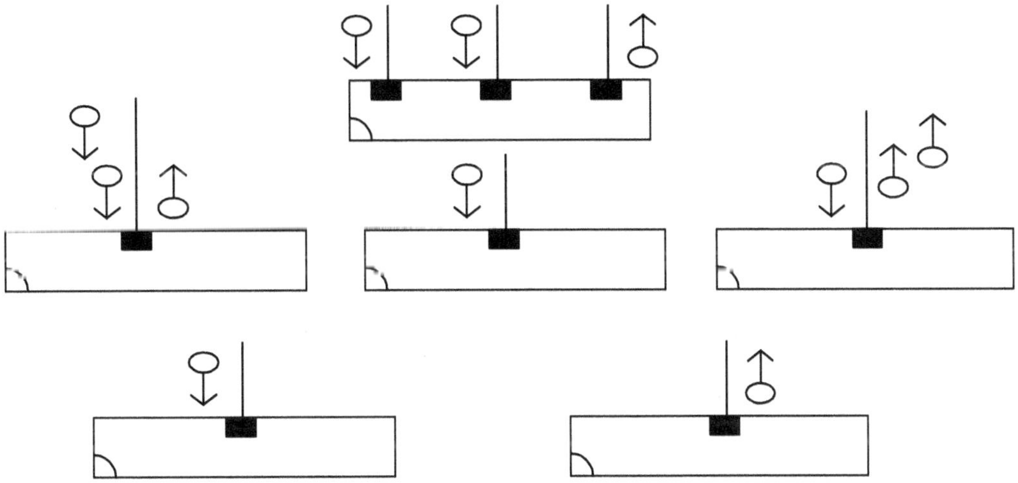

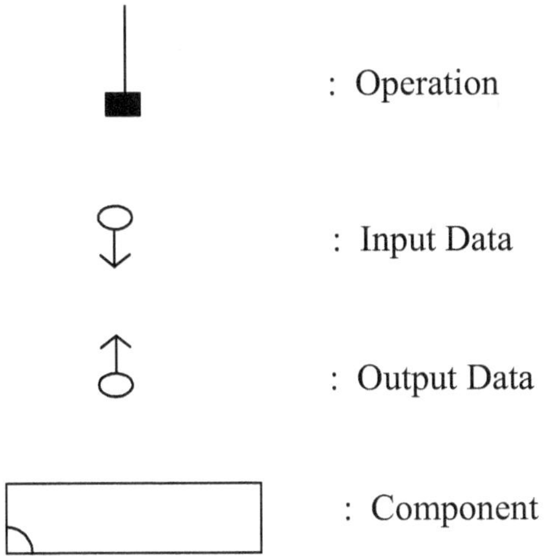
: Operation
: Input Data
: Output Data
: Component

(4) Component Connection Diagram

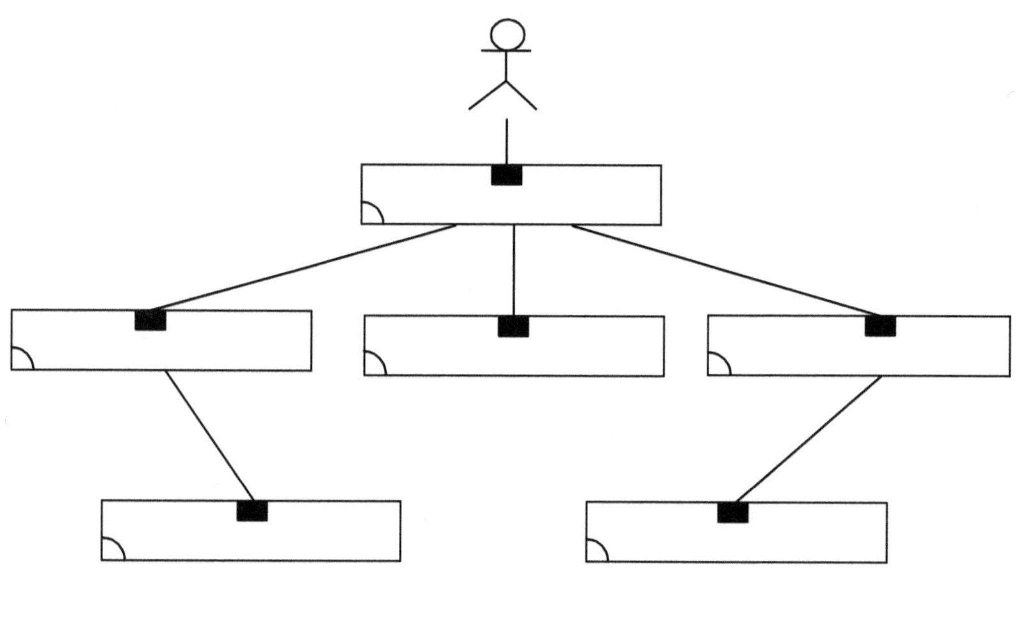

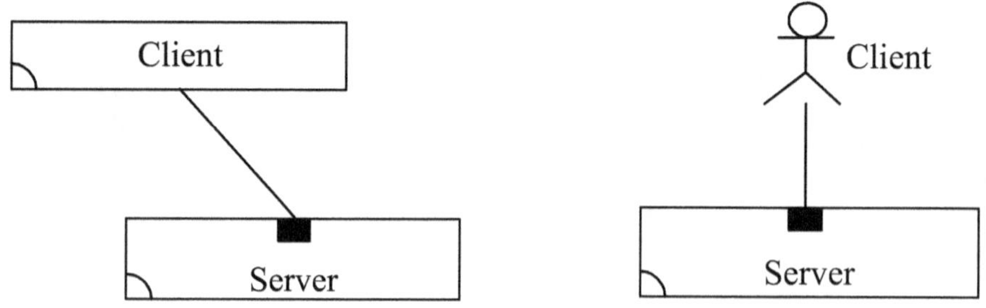

(5) Structure-Behavior Coalescence Diagram

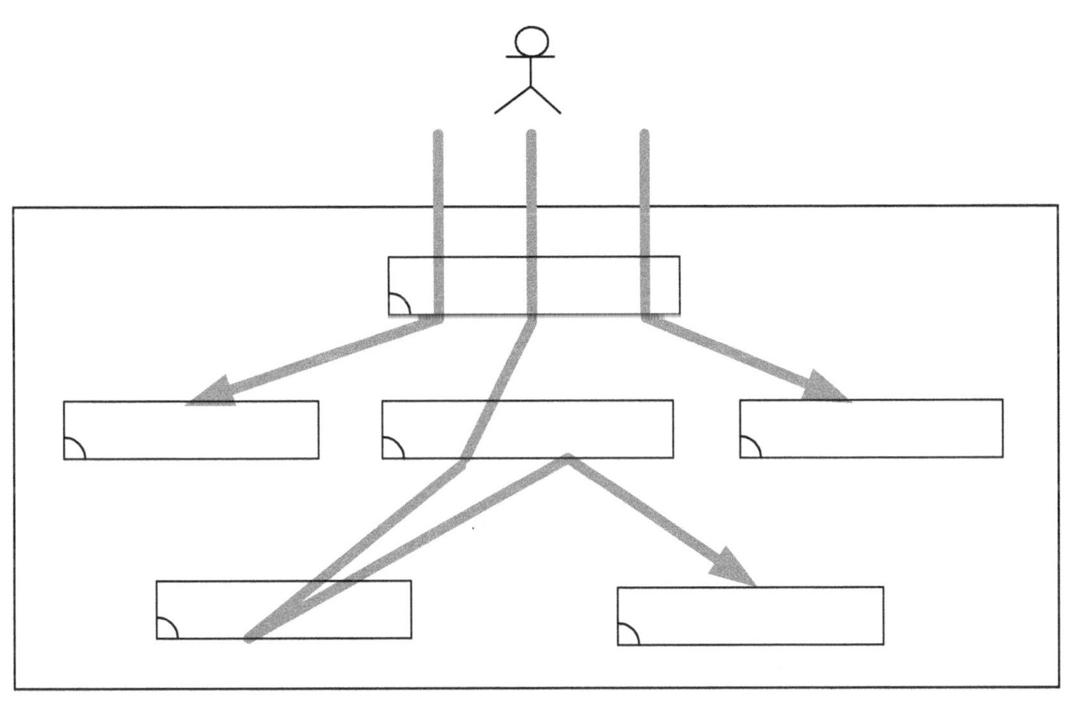

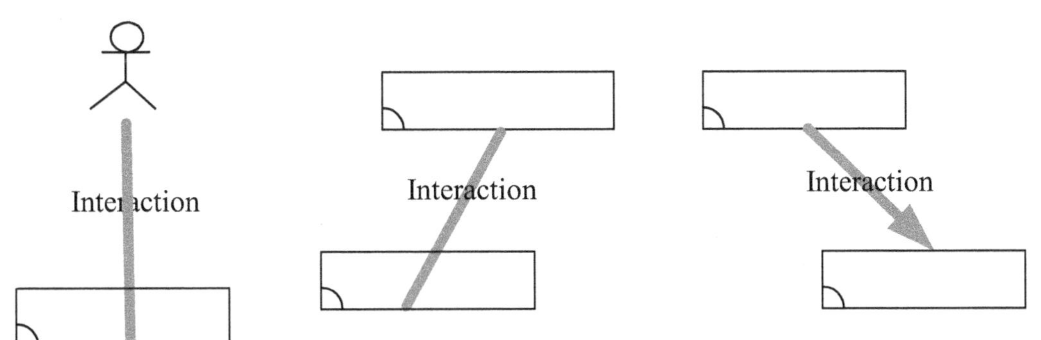

(6) Interaction Flow Diagram

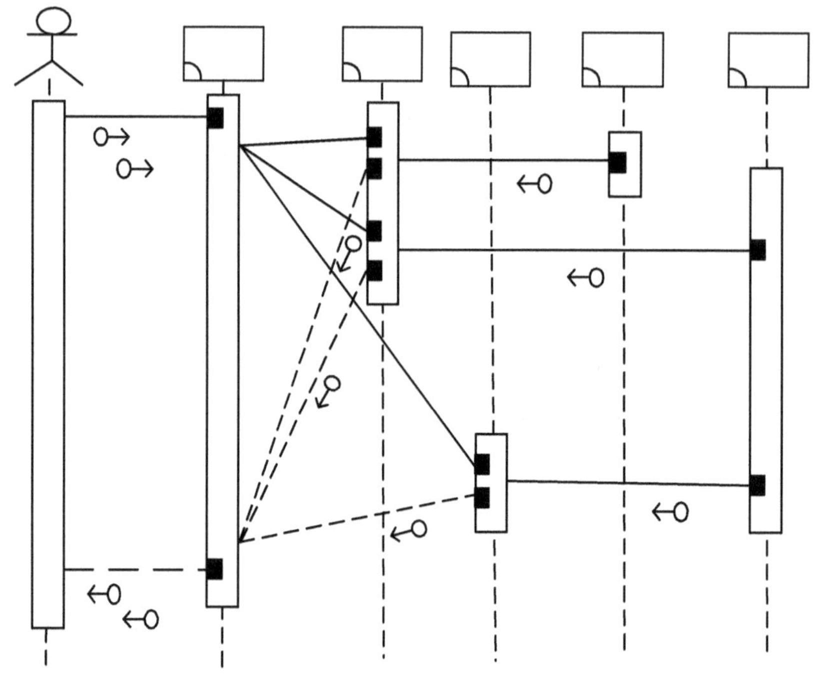

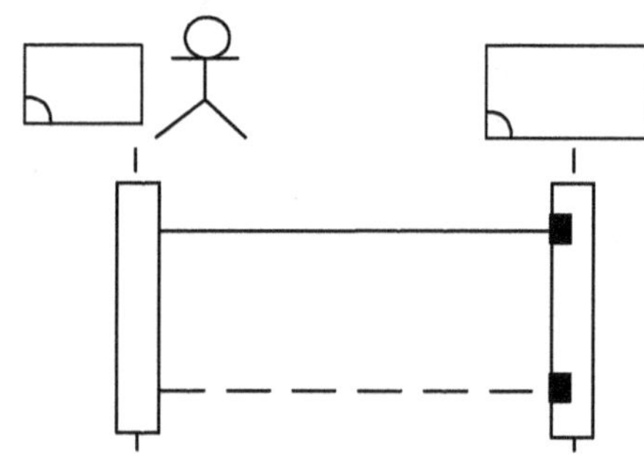

: Operation Call Interaction

: Operation Return Interaction

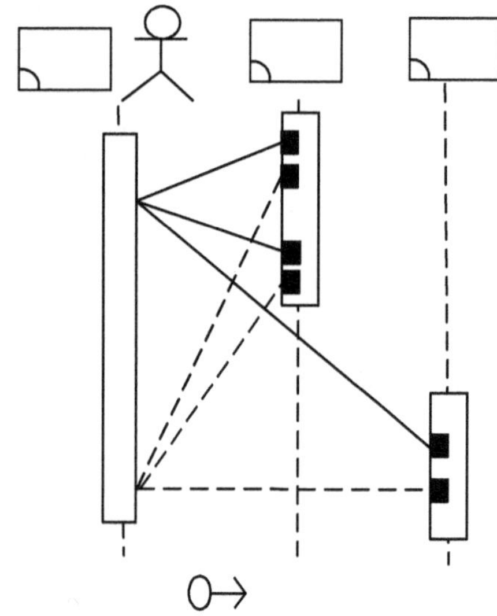

: Conditional
Operation Call Interaction

: Conditional
Operation Return Interaction

: Input Data

: Output Data

APPENDIX B: SBC PROCESS ALGEBRA

(1) Operation-Based Single-Queue SBC Process Algebra

(1) <System> ::= "**fix**(" <Process_Variable> "="<IFD> " • " <Process_Variable>
{"+" <IFD> " • " <Process_Variable>} ")"

(2) <IFD> ::= <Type_1_Interaction> {"• " <Type_1_Or_2_Interaction>}

(3) <Type_1_Or_2_Interaction> ::= <Type_1_Interaction>

| <Type_2_Interaction>

(2) Operation-Based Multi-Queue SBC Process Algebra

(1) <System> ::= <FixIFD> {"|| " <FixIFD>}

(2) <FixIFD> ::= "**fix**(" <Process_Variable>"="<IFD>
"•" <Process_Variable> ")"

(3) <IFD> ::= <Type_1_Interaction> {"• " Type_1_Or_2_Interaction>}

(4) <Type_1_Or_2_Interaction> ::= <Type_1_Interaction>

| <Type_2_Interaction>

(3) Operation-Based Infinite-Queue SBC Process Algebra

(1) <System> ::= "! ("<IFD> " • " *STOP* ")" {"|| ! (" <IFD> " • " *STOP* ")"}

(2) <IFD> ::= <Type_1_Interaction> {"• " <Type_1_Or_2_Interaction>}

(3) <Type_1_Or_2_Interaction> ::= <Type_1_Interaction>

| <Type_2_Interaction>

BIBLIOGRAPHY

[Burd10] Burd, S. D., *Systems Architecture*, 6th Edition, Cengage Learning, 2010.

[Chao14a] Chao, W. S., *Systems Thingking 2.0: Architectural Thinking Using the SBC Architecture Description Language*, CreateSpace Independent Publishing Platform, 2014.

[Chao14b] Chao, W. S., *General Systems Theory 2.0: General Architectural Theory Using the SBC Architecture*, CreateSpace Independent Publishing Platform, 2014.

[Chao14c] Chao, W. S., *Software Modeling and Architecting: Structure-Behavior Coalescence for Software Architecture*, CreateSpace Independent Publishing Platform, 2014.

[Chao15a] Chao, W. S., *A Process Algebra For Systems Architecture: The Structure-Behavior Coalescence Approach*, CreateSpace Independent Publishing Platform, 2015.

[Chao15b] Chao, W. S., *An Observation Congruence Model For Systems Architecture: The Structure-Behavior Coalescence Approach*, CreateSpace Independent Publishing Platform, 2015.

[Chao16] Chao, W. S., *System: Contemporary Concept, Definition, and Language*, CreateSpace Independent Publishing Platform, 2016.

[Chao17a] Chao, W. S., *Channel-Based Single-Queue SBC Process Algebra For Systems Definition: General Architectural Theory at Work*, CreateSpace Independent Publishing Platform, 2017.

[Chao17b] Chao, W. S., *Channel-Based Multi-Queue SBC Process Algebra For Systems Definition: General Architectural Theory at Work*, CreateSpace

Independent Publishing Platform, 2017.

[Chao17c] Chao, W. S., *Channel-Based Infinite-Queue SBC Process Algebra For Systems Definition: General Architectural Theory at Work*, CreateSpace Independent Publishing Platform, 2017.

[Chao17d] Chao, W. S., *Operation-Based Single-Queue SBC Process Algebra For Systems Definition: General Architectural Theory at Work*, CreateSpace Independent Publishing Platform, 2017.

[Chao17e] Chao, W. S., *Operation-Based Multi-Queue SBC Process Algebra For Systems Definition: Unification of Systems Structure and Systems Behavior*, CreateSpace Independent Publishing Platform, 2017.

[Chao17f] Chao, W. S., *Operation-Based Infinite-Queue SBC Process Algebra For Systems Definition: Unification of Systems Structure and Systems Behavior*, CreateSpace Independent Publishing Platform, 2017.

[Chec99] Checkland, P., *Systems Thinking, Systems Practice: Includes a 30-Year Retrospective*, 1st Edition, Wiley, 1999.

[Craw15] Crawley, P. et al., *System Architecture: Strategy and Product Development for Complex Systems*, Prentice Hall, 2015.

[Dam06] Dam, S., *DoD Architecture Framework: A Guide to Applying System Engineering to Develop Integrated Executable Architectures*, BookSurge Publishing, 2006.

[Date03] Date, C. J., *An Introduction to Database Systems*, 8th Edition, Addison Wesley, 2003.

[Denn08] Dennis, A. et al., *Systems Analysis and Design*, 4th Edition, Wiley, 2008.

[Dori95] Dori, D., "Object-Process Analysis: Maintaining the Balance between System Structure and Behavior," *Journal of Logic and Computation* 5(2), pp.227-249, 1995.

[Dori02] Dori, D., *Object-Process Methodology: A Holistic Systems Paradigm*, Springer Verlag, New York, 2002.

[Dori16] Dori, D., *Model-Based Systems Engineering with OPM and SysML*, Springer Verlag, New York, 2016.

[Elma10] Elmasri, R., *Fundamentals of Database Systems*, 6th Edition, Addison Wesley, 2010.

[Hoar85] Hoare, C. A. R., *Communicating Sequential Processes*, Prentice-Hall, 1985.

[Kend10] Kendall, K. et al., *Systems Analysis and Design*, 8th Edition, Prentice Hall, 2010.

[Maie09] Maier, M. W., *The Art of Systems Architecting*, 3rd Edition, CRC Press, 2009.

[Miln89] Milner, R., *Communication and Concurrency*, Prentice-Hall, 1989.

[Miln99] Milner, R., *Communicating and Mobile Systems: the π-Calculus*, 1st Edition, Cambridge University Press, 1999.

[O'Rou03] O'Rourke, C. et al, *Enterprise Architecture Using the Zachman Framework*, 1st Edition, Course Technology, 2003.

[Pele00] Peleg, M. et al., "The Model Multiplicity Problem: Experimenting with Real-Time Specification Methods". *IEEE Tran. on Software Engineering*. 26 (8), pp. 742–759, 2000.

[Prat00] Pratt, T. W. et al., *Programming Languages: Design and Implementation*, 4th Edition, Prentice Hall 2000.

[Pres09] Pressman, R. S., *Software Engineering: A Practitioner's Approach*, 7th Edition, McGraw-Hill, 2009.

[Putm00] Putman, J. R. et al., *Architecting with RM-ODP*, Prentice-Hall, 2000.

[Rayn09] Raynard, B., *TOGAF The Open Group Architecture Framework 100*

Success Secrets, Emereo Pty Ltd, 2009.

[Roza11] Rozanski, N. et al., *Software Systems Architecture: Working With Stakeholders Using Viewpoints and Perspectives*, 2nd Edition, Addison-Wesley Professional, 2011.

[Rumb91] Rumbaugh, J. et al., *Object-Oriented Modeling and Design*, Prentice-Hall, 1991.

[Seth96] Sethi, R., *Programming Languages: Concepts and Constructs*, 2nd Edition, Addison-Wesley, 1996.

[Sode03] Soderborg, N.R. et al., "OPM-based Definitions and Operational Templates," *Communications of the ACM* 46(10), pp. 67-72, 2003.

[Somm06] Sommerville, I., *Software Engineering*, 8th Edition, Addison-Wesley, 2006.

[Toga08] The Open Group, *TOGAF Version 9 - A Manual (TOGAF Series)*, 9th Edition, Van Haren Publishing, 2008.

[Your99] Yourdon, E., *Death March: The Complete Software Developer's Guide to Surviving Mission Impossible Projects*, Prentice-Hall, 1999.

www.ingramcontent.com/pod-product-compliance
Lightning Source LLC
LaVergne TN
LVHW060144070326
832902LV00018B/2948

* 9 7 8 1 9 8 3 4 7 3 6 0 9 *